Critical Essays on Dagaaba Rhetoric

AMERICAN UNIVERSITY STUDIES

SERIES VII
THEOLOGY AND RELIGION

VOL. 295

PETER LANG
New York • Washington, D.C./Baltimore • Bern
Frankfurt am Main • Berlin • Brussels • Vienna • Oxford

Anthony Y. Naaeke

Critical Essays on Dagaaba Rhetoric

PETER LANG
New York • Washington, D.C./Baltimore • Bern
Frankfurt am Main • Berlin • Brussels • Vienna • Oxford

Library of Congress Cataloging-in-Publication Data

Naaeke, Anthony Y.
Critical essays on Dagaaba rhetoric / Anthony Y. Naaeke.
p. cm. — (American University studies VII: Theology and religion; v. 295)
Includes bibliographical references.
1. Rhetoric—Social aspects—Ghana. 2. Dagaare language—Rhetoric.
3. Discourse analysis, Narrative—Ghana. 4. Communication in community development—Ghana. 5. Dagaaba (African people)—Religion.
6. Dagaaba (African people)—Social life and customs. I. Title.
P301.3.G5N33 808'.049365—dc22 2009018148
ISBN 978-1-4331-0680-4
ISSN 0740-0446

Bibliographic information published by **Die Deutsche Nationalbibliothek**.
Die Deutsche Nationalbibliothek lists this publication in the "Deutsche Nationalbibliografie"; detailed bibliographic data is available on the Internet at http://dnb.d-nb.de/.

The paper in this book meets the guidelines for permanence and durability of the Committee on Production Guidelines for Book Longevity of the Council of Library Resources.

29 Broadway, 18th floor, New York, NY 10006
www.peterlang.com

Printed in Germany

To my dearest mother Priscilla

Contents

Preface

This book consists of a collection of essays on various aspects of Dagaaba (African) culture. Each of the essays is a rhetorical analysis of an aspect of Dagaaba culture.

In the course of writing this book, many people or institutions have been of help to me and I am very grateful to them. I am grateful to Peter Lang Publishing for granting me permission to reprint a chapter from my book, *Kaleidoscope Catechesis: Missionary Catechesis in Africa, particularly in the Diocese of Wa in Ghana* (2006). I am also grateful to the *Journal of Dagaare Studies* for granting me permission to reprint some articles that were initially published in that journal. I am equally grateful to the journal *Gender and Behaviour* for giving me permission to reprint two of the articles that have been previously published in that journal.

I am very grateful to Candida M. Saagber and her son, Gustav Balangtaa, who have supported me at various levels of writing this book. On a number of occasions, Candida was my chauffeur to and from the airport when I was scheduled to make a presentation at the Religious Communication Association's pre-convention where many of these articles were presented prior to their publication. Finally, my sincere thanks go to Dr. Gervase Angsotinge, recently retired English literature lecturer at the University of Ghana, Legon, for proof-reading the manuscript.

Anthony Y. Naaeke

Introduction

Rhetoric is not easy to define because its substance and scope encompass many disciplines and situations. Originating from the Greek courts and democracy, rhetoric was seen as an art of persuasive speaking by means of which a person developed arguments to inform and persuade an audience in order to move them to some desired action.

Aristotle defined rhetoric as the art of discovering in any instance the available means of persuasion. (Arist. Bk. 1) The instance could be in the courts (forensic), or in state legislature (deliberative) or in ceremonial occasions (epideictic). Since classical times, the emphasis of rhetoric has often been on the artful use of language to persuade an audience. However, other forms of communication, such as, songs, folktales, ritual, paintings, etc. may equally be persuasive. In light of this, I agree with Kenneth Burke that symbolic action is persuasion that uses both verbal and non-verbal symbols to create a suasory effect on an audience. Hence, rhetoric is present "in physical actions, facial expressions, gestures, and signs." (Ochs 1993, 2; Burke 1966; Kennedy, "A Hoot in the dark, 4)

For Poulakos (1999), "Rhetoric is the art which seeks to capture in opportune moments that which is appropriate and attempts to suggest that which is possible" (Poulakos 1999, 26). Although Poulakos' definition of rhetoric captures the essence of rhetoric as it is conceptualized by Aristotle, I am particularly intrigued by the emphasis on two elements in his definition: "to capture in opportune moments" and "to suggest that which is possible". These two elements highlight the contingent nature of rhetoric as well as its orientation toward action. Through an opportune (kairos) engagement of an event, idea or person, rhetoric prepares the ground for purposeful action. For people to engage in purposeful action there is the need for information and freedom to choose. This means that rhetorical communication presupposes that people are free to make choices based on their personal assessment of available information.

Among the Dagaaba of Ghana rhetorical communication may be said to encompass a gamut of situations: cultural narratives, religious beliefs and rituals, and social and developmental concerns.

Cultural narratives are embodied rhetoric. Narratives tell the story of a community and reflect the shared beliefs and values of a community as they are lived and celebrated in rituals, especially religious rituals. Cultural narratives also express the hopes and dreams of the community.

The essays in the book will introduce the reader to the cultural narratives of the Dagaaba of Ghana and show how community beliefs and values are enacted in ritual celebrations as well as in social movements. Social change and development programs show forth the beliefs and values of a community that are celebrated as epideictic performance and meant to inspire and summon audiences to some form of action. In this light, the essay on the reader-response analysis of an aspect of the *bagre* myth will elucidate and highlight some cultural beliefs and values regarding Dagaaba perception of women, children and a daring spirit. The Dagaaba, like many African societies, are very religious. Religion (African traditional religion and Christianity) permeates every aspect of their life. Because many Dagaaba have embraced Christianity, the essays on missionary activity will introduce the reader to the persuasive function of missionary activity among the Dagaaba and show how Dagaaba are affected by and respond to persuasive messages in religious discourse.

Finally, rhetoric prepares the ground for action. It is essential to social change and social stability. (Luciates et al., 381) Therefore, the essays on domestic violence and the importance of liberating women in African societies fall within the purview of the rhetoric of social change and development communication. In many respects, Dagaaba (African) women are aware of their subjugated position in their culture which is patriarchal. Yet, they are also conscious of alternative ways of life, the attainment of which entails some form of decisive action.

This book is a pioneering effort in expanding the scope of rhetoric beyond those that constitute the mainstream of the discipline. As an entry point into Dagaaba rhetoric, a book of this size will not only be easy to read but it will also be a stimulus for further research.

The essays in this book have been previously presented at scholarly conferences or published. I am grateful to the editors of the *Journal of Dagaare Studies* and *Gender and Behaviour* for granting me permission to reprint essays that were originally published in those journals.

References

Aristotle. *The Rhetoric and Poetics*. Translated by W. Rhys Roberts. New York: McGraw Hill, 1984.

Burke, Kenneth. *Language as Symbolic Action: Essays on Life, Literature, and Method*. Berkeley, CA: University of California Press, 1966.

Kennedy, George A. "A hoot in the dark: The evolution of general rhetoric," *Philosophy and Rhetoric*, 25, 1992.

Luciates, L. John, Condit M. Celeste, Sally Caudill. (Eds.). *Contemporary Rhetorical Theory: a reader*. New York/London: The Guilford Press, 1999.

Ochs, Donovan J. *Consolatory rhetoric: grief, symbol, and ritual in the Greco-Roman era*. Columbia, SC: University of South Carolina Press, 1993.

Poulakos, John. "Toward a sophistic definition of rhetoric," in *Contemporary rhetorical theory: a reader*. Edited by Luciates, Condit, and Sally, Columbia, SC: University of South Carolina Press, 1999.

Chapter 1
The Dagaaba of Ghana

This chapter was originally published in *Kaleidoscope catechesis: missionary catechesis in northwestern Ghana*. It is reprinted with permission of Peter Lang Publishing.

The Dagaaba reside in the Upper West Region of Ghana which covers the districts of Wa, Lawra, Tumu, Jirapa-Lambusie, and Nadowli. The Upper West region was created in January 1983 and officially inaugurated on September 28, 1987, by the Chairman of the then ruling Provisional National Defense Council (PNDC), Fl. Lt. Jerry J. Rawlings. Prior to this date, it was administered as part of the Upper Region with its headquarters at Bolgatanga. The region shares a common border with la Cote d'Ivoire in the West, Burkina Faso in the North and the Upper East and Northern regions to the East and South, respectively. It occupies about 18,500 square kilometers, which represent approximately 7.8 per cent of Ghana's total landmass of 258,538 square kilometers. The region is home to about 450, 000 people, about four per cent of Ghana's total population. About 90 per cent of the region is rural.

The three main tribes of the area are the Dagaaba, Sisaala, and Wala. The Wala are mostly Muslim. Other ethnic groups are the Birifor, Manlaale and Chakale. The main dialects spoken are Dagaare, Sisaali and Wali. The dominant tribes that have embraced Christianity are the Dagaaba and the Sisaala. These two tribal groups share many common cultural practices and religious beliefs, as Edward Tengan so clearly explains in his book, *Land as Being and Cosmos: the Institution of the Earth Cult among the Sisaala of Northwestern Ghana*. (Tengan 43) The Manlaale, Birifor and Chakale dialects are closely related to Dagaare. However, I will use Dagaaba in this study to include the Birifor and Chakale.

Dagaaba social organization is characterized by a low degree of role and institutional specialization. Apart from a few specialized roles, such as, *diviner*, people generally learn to do whatever work is necessary for the upkeep of family or community. Tradition is cherished, and elders have the responsibility to protect the time-honored axioms and mores (Mendonsa 36) of past generations.

In this region, unilineal descent groups are widely dispersed among peoples of different language and social organization. Compounds are scattered unevenly across the countryside in such a way that it is difficult to tell where one settlement ends and the next begins. (Goody 17)

The two main tribes, which were the original focus of missionary activity from 1929 until recently, when parishes were opened among the Birifor and the Chakale, were the Dagaaba and the Sisaala. Some amount of study on the social and religious world-view of the Dagaaba and Sisaala has been done by expert ethnographers, anthropologists and theologians, such as, Henri Labouret (1931), Robert S. Rattray (1932), L Girault (1959), Jack Goody (1967), Bruce Grindal (1972), Eugene Mendonsa (1982), Edward Kuukure (1985), Edward Tengan (1991), Paul Bekye (1991), Alexis Tengan (2000) and Eugene Suom-Dery (2000). Since this is not an ethnographic or anthropological study of the various tribes in the Upper West Region only those aspects of Dagaaba world-view that shed light on the religious discourse and ritual, narratives and social action will be considered and accentuated.

Geographically, the land occupied by the Dagaaba is flat with low trees. The year is divided into two distinct seasons - dry and wet - the latter lasting from late April through October. Temperatures range between 20 and 35 degrees Celsius.

The people who live in this area are mainly subsistence farmers. They derive their livelihood from cultivating the land and rearing animals. Farming is done by means of a hoe, although animal traction has been introduced by agricultural projects funded by government and the Catholic Church. Cereal crops, such as guinea-corn, maize and millet, and shoot crops, such as, groundnuts and yams, are cultivated. Livestock include cattle, sheep, goats, dogs, chickens and guinea fowls. Fruits include dawa-dawa, baobab and sheanuts. Sheanuts are particularly popular because they contain oil, which is easily extracted for domestic use.

For art and craft, some people weave baskets using reeds picked up along the riverbanks. Others engage in blacksmithing and still others make xylophones or carve wood. Some women make clay pots and brew beer (*pito*).

Before the advent of the British colonizers, the Dagaaba were not organized as a political society in the same way that other African societies, such as, the Asante in Southern Ghana, were. Chieftaincy among the Dagaaba was, therefore, a political imposition by the British colonial masters. The Dagaare word for chief, *naa,* means "either a chief or wealthy person." (Angsotinge 102) The chiefs were responsible for enforcing the law imposed by the colonial administration in their respective villages and also for collecting taxes from the people for the colonial government.

Prior to the advent of the colonial administration, the main source of traditional authority was the *tendaana* or *tengan sob* (custodian of the land) and village elders. The *tendaana* and village elders wielded socio-religious power and authority. The *tendaana* or *tengan sob* is usually chosen from the clan that first settled in an area. Among the Dagaaba, the *tenggan sob* is a priest or custodian of the shrine that is dedicated to the spirit of the earth.

Because the Dagaaba did not have an organized political system does not mean that they were a lawless people. Dagaaba society is organized around the clan.

Clan members are those who share a common birth-origin. They trace their descent to a common male ancestor whose name may even be lost to surviving members. The whole clan is a family, and members have reciprocal responsibilities toward other members of the clan. In clanship relations, seniority by age is the general rule in the exercise of authority. Decisions are usually reached through discussion and informal consensus among the elders.

Dagaaba Anthropology

I base this section on the research findings of Jack Goody, Edward Kuukure, Edward Tengan, Gbaane Dabire, Bekuone Some Deri, and Suom-Dery, just to mention a few authors who have researched Dagaaba culture. It should be pointed out that research in this field is still at its infancy.

The human person or man (used in its generic form) is *bon-biila, bon-banguura* (a puzzle, enigma). It is not easy to know and understand every intricacy about man. According to Dagaaba mythologies, man was either created or appeared out of the earth. Then, the serpent taught male and female how to copulate and beget offspring. Suom-Dery (2000) summarizes Dagaaba anthropology as follows:

> divine origin of the total man, the creation of man as male and female orientated to marriage and to the family life, the pre-existence and sacredness of human life, the uniqueness of the individual by virtue of his name, the Dagara attitude to human sexuality and their view of man as a learning being, the place of cultural creativity. (Suom-Dery 64)

For some African cultures, including the Dagaaba, man is a composite unit of body and spirit, an organic whole as against a Greek philosophical conception of man as a rational and dualistic being composed of body and soul. Among the Dagaaba, for instance, *Nisaale* (man) distinguishes a human being from an animal while *Nir* connotes an actualized *Nisaale* (human being) with human and moral qualities of which Dagaaba are proud or to which they aspire. (Kuukure 83; Suom-Dery 65) The body of man is animated by *vuuro* or *nyovur* (breath or nose-breath) drained by *zii* (blood) pumped by the *sukyir* (heart) which is located inside the body. Without *vuuro* the body is lifeless. *Zii* not only sustains the body, it also defines a person in relation to others. It identifies a person with a network of kinship. *Sukyir* is the seat of emotions, feelings and thought besides its biological function. It is therefore a source of decision-making and action.

There are also immaterial elements of the human being. They are *ya* (mind, reason, intelligence, sense, faculty of moral judgment) and *sie* (spirit-soul). (Suom-Dery 66) The *sie* is the seat of sudden emotions and makes the material or physical body become a person (*Nir*). Without entering into detail about the specific nature and characteristics of *sie* as Goody and Kuukure have done, it suffices to mention that the separation of the body and *sie* indicates physical death. However, shortly after death, the *sie* continues to live first as *nyaakpiin* (ghost) and then as *kpiin* (spirit) as it journeys to, and eventually becomes a member of the spirits in *kpimeteng* (land of the dead).

In Dagaaba anthropology man is also composed of an element called *deor* or *degr* (dirt, impurity). It is a mystical quality that a person contracts through multiple relations with other human beings and nature.

In summary, man is a composite being of body and soul, *yan* and *vuuro*, *sie* and *degr*. I have left out *dasule* (shadow) from this list because I consider *dasule* to be a part of *sie*. He is a unity of all these parts, a conscious and responsible self capable of relating with others. (Kuukure 83; Suom-Dery 72)

For Dagaaba to be a person is to be in relationship with others and the deity within time and history. The most basic unit of human relationships is the family born out of marriage.

Marriage among the Dagaaba

Traditionally, marriage assures both the continuity of life and the cohesion of the social group. For the Dagaaba marriage is understood as a stable union between families and clans. This does not mean that family and clan relations interfere with the private conjugal life of married couples. Marriage is seen as a social obligation, a factor of individual and collective (lineage) survival and as a sign of moral and social equilibrium. A healthy unmarried adult man is an object of derision and shame.

Before marriage, arrangements are completed and guardianship of the bride is transferred to the clan of the groom. This transfer of rights over the woman is accompanied by a transfer of property (bride wealth/price), which is essential for a valid marriage.

Polygamy is allowed in Dagaaba marriage. Levirate marriage is one of the main reasons for polygamy. When a man dies, one of his brothers or nearest of kin in the male lineage inherits the widow, unless she decides to go away. If a man's wife is sterile, the whole clan will feel concerned and will seek to persuade him to get a second wife to ensure the growth of the clan and to save the first marriage. Also, it is quite normal for a woman to encourage her husband to take another wife so that she can have a helpmate in the domestic chores. People glory in having many children and this is probably one other reason for polygamy. Having many children also raises the social status of the family concerned. It ensures that there will be more hands to help in time of need. It also helps to prevent or reduce adultery and prostitution, especially on the part of the husband.

Divorce is not common. Once the full contract of marriage has been executed, it is "extremely hard to dissolve it." (Kuukure 31) This is probably because marriage is seen as a process which is complete when several children have been born and when all the marriage prestations have been made. The reasons for divorce include sterility or barrenness (unless saved by marriage of a second wife), failure of a man to support his wife with food, shelter, health care and ritual accomplishments. Other reasons for divorce are continued cruelty or physical abuse by the husband, the practice (and suspicion) of magic and witchcraft on the part of the wife, inability or refusal to fulfill a wife's allotted economic, domestic and sexual obligations. Temporary separations between husband and wife are more common than divorce.

Religion

The existence of God is an unquestionable reality in the religious worldview of the Dagaaba. Dagaaba also believe in the existence of many spirits. These spirits, which are god's agents, have specific functions for man and society. Dagaaba have myths and stories that try to explain the origins of the world and men, the mysteries of birth and death, and the activities of celestial and mundane beings. The most common and popular myth is the *bagre* myth that has been studied and published by Jack Goody. (1972) The invisible and visible world of the living and the dead dovetail, overlap or even interpenetrate one another, and there is a unity in creation.

Rain Shrine

The rain shrine is found in many Dagaaba houses. It takes a variety of forms. The most common and well-known is the *saa-da-wera*, usually installed near the house, particularly in the *siman* (midden). (Kuukure 62) The rain shrine consists of a stock driven into the ground; a peg about a foot long carved out of a tree that has been struck by lightning is transfixed through a hole in this stock, in the form of a cross. An evil in the family, such as, sickness, can occasion the installation of this shrine.

The rain shrine is universally of great significance in oaths and similar procedures. The killing power of lightning is something the Dagaaba dread, and death from "rain" is always attributed to some major offense against the shrine. (62)

Rain has the function of procuring the fecundity of the land. Hence, the head of the family makes a sacrifice to the rain shrine before cultivation of the fields to ask a blessing and protection on all those who work on the farm. At the end of the cultivation, a thanksgiving sacrifice is offered by the *tendaana* either during the annual harvest festival or at the request of an individual or family.

Earth Shrine

The earth shrine is the most important focus of religious activity. Through its cult the village emerges as a social unit. Dagaaba, for example, believe that the earth shrine has a mystical or supernatural force called *tengan tiib*. This force is represented by a totem (*tiib*) which is usually placed or built in a thick grove (*tengan tug*). At the *tengan tug*, sacrifices are offered to the *tengan*. (Angsotinge 88-89) The earth shrine provides sanctions against interpersonal aggression (bloodshed and witchcraft), against self-destruction (suicide), against depletion of the community (sale of members), and thievery. It also places some control upon sexuality. (Kuukure 64) The *tengan* can be implored as an agent to place a curse on one's enemies. This is done by throwing some dust from *tengan* on the person to be cursed. (Angsotinge 92) The powers of *tengan* are, however, limited to a particular settlement. The *tengan* has no power over a person who does not belong to a settlement over which the *tengan* exercises its domain. (91)

Among the Dagaaba the earth shrine is guarded by the *tendaana* (custodian of the earth shrine). The *tendaana* is the first person to have settled in a previously uninhabited part of the area. The *tendaana* performs ritual sacrifices on behalf of the *tengan*. He also apportions land to new settlers and adjudicates in disputes between people within his geographical jurisdiction. As custodian of the land, the *tendaana* "receives all lost property that has been found in his area and that has not been claimed" (88-89). This includes unclaimed corpses that may be found on the land in his care. The *tendaana* supervises economic activities of the area in his charge, particularly the village market (*daa*) which serves many purposes. Village markets are places where people go to sell and buy commodities and to rendezvous with friends. They are also places where information of a public nature is easily disseminated among the people.

The *tendaana* performs ritual and religious roles in his area. He offers sacrifice for various reasons. A major reason a *tendaana* offers sacrifice is for "intercession and expiation." (101) After harvest, he also offers a sacrifice of thanksgiving.

Ancestors or Ancestor Spirits (*Kpime*)

Ancestor veneration (not worship) is an important ritual function among the Dagaaba. An ancestor is a deceased elder who lived a good and exemplary life on earth and, upon his death, becomes a member of the eternal beings. Not everyone qualifies to be an ancestor. The ancestors are dead human beings who have been transformed into spiritual agencies and who have spiritual jurisdiction over their lineage kin and, in limited ways, to their matrilateral descendants.

For the Dagaaba parenthood is a prerequisite for having an ancestor shrine carved in one's name. The second prerequisite is a proper death as distinct from an evil one. Death is considered evil if it was the result of suicide, leprosy or insanity. Only males who have children born in their name may have a shrine carved in their name. It is the male child who is said to be responsible for carving the shrine of his father. However, there are cases when the daughter can prevail upon her paternal uncle, the dead man's full brother, to perform the required rites on her behalf and create a shrine for her dead father.

Men who die childless or who have suffered an evil death are denied an ancestor shrine unless the sin that has been committed is first expiated by the prescribed sacrifices. The killing of a fellow clansman is an unforgivable offense against the ancestors, and a shrine is never carved for a man who kills his father or brother. A woman who has left children behind her also has a shrine established in her name. An ancestor must have been well esteemed by the community. (Kuukure 65–66) The wicked, especially witches, never get to become ancestors.

Guardian Spirits

Dagaaba believe in spirits. The first and foremost of these is the earth shrine itself. Each clan has its spirit guardian, although linked clans may have the same one. The altar is usually different for each local clan sector. Like the belief in a totemic animal, which is also sometimes spoken of as a spirit guardian, this concept is associated with the patrilineal descent group. Each individual has a guardian spirit. Each group has a selection of possible guardian spirits available to its members, including the spirit guardian of the clan itself, individual ancestors, and usually the most important medicine shrines of the lineage. (68)

Medicine shrines

Medicine shrines refer to any of the thousands of multi-purpose private and personal shrines. These shrines are mostly placed outside the house. They are made from sticks, stones, clay pots and calabashes. (68) There is a proliferation of medicine shrines and they are used for the protection of their adherents, for the restoration of health, for success in war or hunting and for casting spells for good and bad, preventive and curative. Medicine shrines may have been inherited, acquired at the instruction of a diviner, discovered in connection with the wild-bush and with the possession and inspiration of the "beings of the wild" or some spirit. Or they may have been sought or even bought on the initiative of the present owner as remedy for some social, psychological or physical misfortune. All medicine shrines have histories of migration or acquisition from within or without the geographical area. (69) Each has its particular taboos and demands of sacrifices and offerings.

Beings of the Wild/Fairies

In sculpture, the shrines of these beings consist of a representation of a male and female spoken of as dwarf-like creatures having human appearance. Yet seldom does anyone get to see them. According to Dagaaba, beings of the wild speak with a high pitch and nasal accent. They are believed to have descended from above, from god and are god's children and messengers with powers derived from him. Apparently, they can reproduce their kind. Not only are they always represented as a couple, they are said to have children. They are believed to inhabit the hills, rivers and trees. (71) All knowledge of supernatural agencies comes from these beings of the wild. They are indispensable for the diviner, when he is consulted by a client. On the other hand these beings appear to be very difficult to handle. Those who use them will make gains, but they are also bound to offer whatever religious duty they demand. The failure to do this or a breach of their taboo will be severely punished with beating and anything else, not excluding death.

When they are angry, the man who contains them becomes eccentric and behaves like a mad beast. The *kontome* cannot be exorcised. They can, however, be calmed down by being accepted, making a shrine to them, and offering the duty or ritual they want.

Economic World-view

Economically, Northwestern Ghana, where Dagaaba reside, has been the underdog as far as Ghana's development endeavor is concerned. In no part of Ghana are the problems of under-development so concentrated and so focused as in the Northwest. The people here are beset with many maladies and crises: poor rains, poor crop yields, inadequate schools to accommodate the teeming youthful populations, poor sanitary conditions and lack of potable water. One can hardly talk of a "per capita" income when the majority of people in these areas have virtually no incomes. Substandard living is pervasive in many of these rural communities. (Bekye 42) It is no secret that the area largely still lags behind the rest of the country in terms of the provisions of many basic and necessary amenities, facilities and services. Consequently, many Dagaaba migrate to southern Ghana in search of jobs.

Although migration, per se, can be viewed as a manifestation of initiative and enterprise, its effects on basically agrarian rural populations, dependent on human labor supply, can sometimes be disastrous for the migrant, the family and community that he leaves behind. Migration usually entails family separation, exposure to different cultural values and adoption of new ways of perceiving the world. Sometimes it entails the acquisition of bad habits, contraction of deadly diseases (especially AIDS), and adoption of, or association with, alien ritual practices that often rival the migrant's traditional gods or spirits.

Despite these inherent problems associated with out-migration, all the mothers, fathers, maternal uncles and other older people agree with the young people themselves that migration is necessary. It is through migration that one's economic situation may improve. The farming communities, in which every able-bodied resident man and woman is a farmer, do not regard farming as work in the general sense; and the compulsion to migrate is regarded, though this is seldom overtly emphasized, as mainly due to lack of lucrative non-farming occupations.

Migration involves permanent or semi-permanent changes in residence and takes into account factors that intervene between the economic opportunities and social conditions of the place of origin and those of the destination. In urban areas, migrants are exposed to better health-care facilities, education and welfare services. There is also the lure of "city lights" and urban excitement. However, migrants miss the traditional African rural life, with its creative entertainment, exciting rituals and vibrant arts and crafts that cumulatively spell their identity.

Festivals and Ceremonies

Festivals mean a lot to Africans because they are an expression of culture and tradition. They are usually held to express appreciation to the deity for good harvest and other blessings received from god. On important occasions, such as, child naming, puberty, marriage and death, certain rites and rituals are performed to mark the occasion. This usually brings the whole village and community together for reunification. Festivals and ritual celebrations, therefore, perform both religious and social functions.

The common features and beliefs expressed in festivals in many African societies are belief in a Supreme Being, life after death and nearness of the ancestors to their living descendants. Festivals are occasions when past leaders of the land, village or tribe are remembered, honored and their help and protection sought. Festivals are times for ritual purification of the land so that people can enter a new season with confidence and hope. Festivals are occasions to display cultural art and affirm cultural values.

The main traditional festivals celebrated in Northwestern Ghana are the *Dumba* festival among the Wala, the *Kobina* festival in Lawra traditional area and the *Kakube* festival of the Nandom traditional area. These festivals are agricultural thanksgiving ceremonies to god for good harvest, protection from enemy aggression and divine blessing upon the people of the particular area. They are also an opportunity for indigenous people to come together to celebrate their cultural heritage through sacrifice, libation, music, dance and drumming. Dancing to folk music, accompanied by *dalare* (tomtom drums) and xylophone, usually moves crowds to excitement and makes everyone express their joy and thanksgiving by joining in singing and dancing. At these ceremonies new songs are composed to express thanks to god. They also depict social problems and call on people to desist from the problems identified, such as, alcoholism, irresponsible parenthood, thievery or diseases. At the end of the festivals, people return home singing the new songs and are obviously being alerted by the songs to social problems that need to be avoided.

Festivals are usually marked by durbars of traditional authority, the chiefs, who display cultural attire by their dress and majestic walking with the elders around them.

Traditional festivals are also occasions for poetry recitals, usually by the youth, singing, dancing and display of art and craft. Festival grounds constitute a snapshot of traditional culture.

The *Bagre* Association

The *bagre* association is a religious community into which a person is initiated through the *bagre* ritual. Scholarly research on the *bagre* association and myth has been done by Jack Goody (1972) and Alexis Tengan (2006). Goody's work on the *Bagre* association and myth is so detailed that no elaboration is necessary here. It just suffices to acknowledge that the association is an important religious and socio-cultural event among the Dagaaba.

Divination

Diviners, sorcerers, oracles, magicians and mediums are an integral part of African societies. These people are specialists in various areas of human life. People consult these specialists with their anxieties and fears.

The diviner has a pre-eminent place in traditional African society. He claims the ability to penetrate the invisible world of the spirits and the dead. He also claims ability to discern and interpret the dispositions and attitudes of the spirits in respect to the living. He is, therefore, the link between the physical and spiritual worlds.

The office of the diviner is given by god (*ngmen*). (Kuukure 102–106; Bekye 185) A person knows that he has been selected by god to be a diviner when he begins to experience strange and abnormal occurrences in the form of bad dreams, frequent sickness, recurrent deaths in the family or lack of productivity in his work. When such abnormal occurrences happen to a person, he usually consults a practicing diviner to find out the cause. When the diviner determines that the spirit of divination is at work, arrangements are made with senior diviners of the area, who come together to install the affected person in his home as a diviner in his own right. He is given the necessary tools for divination: *kontonbilii* (statuettes of the beings of the wild), who reveal to the diviner what goes on in the spirit world and the particular dispositions of individual spirits and the *bagbug-wuo* (divination bag).

The diviner carries out divination in order to solve the problems of people who approach him for help. In traditional African societies nothing happens without a cause. There is hardly a natural occurrence. Diviners are usually consulted to reveal the causes of mishaps that a person may suffer.

Prayers and Sacrifices

Edward Kuukure (1985) and Paul Bekye (1991) have done an excellent job of compiling prayers offered at various shrines and for various purposes. These prayers reveal the spiritual and material concerns of the people who offer them. They also reveal a sense of trust in god, the *tibe* and the readiness of person in prayer to be faithful to the terms of his prayer request.

The prayers are usually for various needs, from community needs to private needs. They express gratitude as well as supplication.

Post-burial Ceremonies

Dagaaba perform elaborate ritual ceremonies after the burial of a deceased member of the family. Kuukure (1985) has described these ceremonies in detail in *The Destiny of Man: Dagaaba Beliefs in Dialogue with Christian Eschatology* (118-119). It is important to remark that the rituals surrounding death among the Dagaaba celebrate their values and beliefs.

Communication Methods among the Dagaaba

In predominantly oral cultures of many African societies, communication is basically oral, ritual and symbolic. Information, messages and knowledge are shared by word of mouth, songs (sacred and secular), funeral dirges, stories, myths, fables, proverbs, riddles or through signs and symbols, as well as art (paintings, weaving) and body language.

Dagaaba generally communicate by word of mouth through words, songs, stories, and dirges. Both positive and negative messages may be expressed by means of oral communication. Messages may also be communicated orally through names. Many Dagaaba names communicate a message about the individual or his family or the circumstances surrounding his birth or even express a wish or affirmation about a thing or person. For example, *Domegyiele* (enemies are envious, or enemies will be envious) communicates a message about a success story in the life of a person or his family that could be a source of envy for the one considered to be an enemy. Another name, *Nbelenyin* (where should I look?) is a name that communicates some form of frustration or desperation. Where should I look? does not only ask a question but also expresses a situation in which a person finds himself at the crossroads of life and seeks direction or help in order to follow the right path.

There are also theophoric names that speak about God and his attributes or express human expectations or affirmations about God. *Mwinbangme* (God knows me) expresses confidence in a personal God who knows the individual. *Angsomwin* (who owns God?) literally affirms that God is a God of all people. He is a universal God.

Songs

Dagaaba love to sing for various reasons and at various occasions. Music is a pastime, a form of entertainment, or a channel to communicate a message that one would find difficult to communicate via another channel. Songs serve a didactic role besides the other functions just mentioned. They teach moral lessons to children and elders alike. A popular didactic song among the Dagaaba is entitled *Nipkee fola* (anxious elder, shameless elder, selfish elder). This song speaks about an elder who eats food while children watch. This song teaches elders to consider the needs of children before their own and to be conscious of giving a good example to the youth.

As a pastime, songs are sung while people work. For example, women grinding at the mill usually sing as pastime but often to express their frustrations or disappointments. Usually, someone in the family would overhear the song and in that way the message is communicated that the woman is not happy about something. They would then ask what she was singing about, and sometimes she would deny the reason she sang a particular song or would express the pain in her heart.

Some songs are sung for ritual purposes. They relate to the sacred expressing human needs, frustrations or reliance on the help of God. They may also express the desire for mercy and pardon.

Funeral dirges are another form of music. They set a tone and create an atmosphere of mourning. Funeral dirges usually describe the qualities and successes of the deceased or his/her living relatives. By listening to funeral dirges, one can know more about the life and work of the deceased and the family to which he belonged.

Proverbs are another form of communication among Dagaaba. Proverbs are used to express a message in a metaphorical way. For instance, *aa wule bibile wob?* (who shows an elephant to a child?). (Bangnikon, 1999; Suom-Dery 485) The elephant is self-evident so that a child will recognize it as soon it sees one. In the same way, certain things (good or bad) are self-evident, such that the child will know when it encounters them. Fire, for instance, will burn the child or anyone if one is not careful so, if a child refuses to listen to the advice of elders, such a proverb is invoked on him. The proverb also teaches that one learns by experience.

The use of proverbs is a sign that one has been successfully socialized into Dagaare cultural expression. It is also a sign of wisdom because of one's ability to use language in a didactic and pithy manner. (218) Proverbs are short and effective tools of communication because they speak directly to the mind and heart of the addressee and call upon him to reflect on the message contained therein and to respond appropriately.

Stories, myths, legends, etc. are all channels of communication among Dagaaba. They teach about the history of the people, their moral values and cultural ideals. They are also a form of entertainment. A compilation of Dagaaba stories has been done by Bemile, Sebastian K. (1983), Kuwabong Dannabang (1992), and Gervase Angsotinge (1986).

Myths are re-acted in annually recurrent festivals, in a rhythm which forms the cosmic framework of space and time. The myths span the whole of existence, from heaven to the hut and the heart of the individuals: in fact, from cosmos to clan.

Body Language

Dagaaba also communicate via body language. They do this through dance, eye contact, gestures and other forms of body movements. To understand and interpret body language requires knowledge and familiarity with the cultural context and modes of expression. A head-nod means agreement or consent while a head-shake indicates disagreement. When a parent looks at a child sternly that is supposed to communicate disagreement to the child.

Dance may express joy or sorrow. The form of dance is determined by the circumstance. The way people dance to express joy during festivals is different from the kind of dance performed at the funeral of an elderly person. Ability to perform the appropriate dance indicates the degree of socialization into the culture.

Drums and xylophones are also used to communicate. The way in which drums or xylophones are played communicates particular messages that a well-socialized person in the culture would understand and correctly interpret.

Signs and Symbols

Symbols communicate messages to people who use them. They are culturally situated although there may be cross-cultural similarity in the use and interpretation of symbols. Symbols can be signs, objects, images, sounds, gestures and persons (Suom-Dery 228) that evoke and warrant appropriate responses from those who understand them and for whom they are significant. A symbol may express something mysterious whose presence or existence, while still beyond the grasp of our rational mind, may be sensed in a way that is simultaneously internal but distant. According to Suom-Dery, the Dagara (singular of Dagaaba) child is born into a symbolic world and house of symbols. (229) Ashes and water, for example, are symbols of peace and reconciliation among the Dagaaba.

Art and Sculpture

Dagaaba also communicate through art and sculpture. By means of art works, such as, baskets, clay pots, hats, decorations on calabashes (gourds cut in half for drinking), carvings, buildings, tombs, etc. beauty is communicated. Other messages may also be communicated through art and sculpture. The message usually depends on the artist.

Writing

With the introduction of formal education by European colonialists and missionaries, a number of Dagaaba have become literate, capable of reading and writing. Dagaare stories, myths, proverbs, songs and history are being committed to writing. Dagaaba scholars write on various aspects of their culture. These documents describe and interpret their indigenous culture, correct erroneous perceptions of their culture by other writers and introduce these people and their cultures to the literary world. A cross-cultural study and interpretation of certain aspects of Dagaaba culture alongside other cultures show great similarities either in expression or mindset. An example is the cosmological, anthropological and religious worldview of the *Bagre* myth considered alongside other myths from the Ancient Near East, the Aborigines of Australia or even the Native American tribal myths and folk narratives. (Kennedy 83)

Religious Communication among Dagaaba

Dagaaba are religious. Religion permeates and influences every aspect of their lives from birth to death and beyond. One can hardly distinguish between the sacred and profane. The elements that constitute the religious world-view of Dagaaba also serve as channels of communication between human beings and God. The nature of communication that goes on between people and the spirit world does not only affect divine-human relationship, it also influences interpersonal and group communication among Dagaaba.

The ancestors, for instance, are not just moral symbols; they are also channels of communication between human beings and God. People send their messages to God through the ancestors or the divinities or spirits or diviners. They do so through prayer, sacrifice (usually animal sacrifice), pouring of libation, or some other ritual performance relating to life or death, such as, the *bagre* initiation or funeral rites.

Although the conception of an ancestor is not uniform among all Dagaaba the fact of their being a channel of communication is not disputed (Suom-Dery 100). The following prayer, said in front of ancestral shrines, shows the mediatory role of the ancestors:

> We ask you (our ancestors) to present our offering to him (*Naabile-ngmen*). We offer it to him with one hand but may he kindly accept it with both hands. (Kpiebaya 62; Kuukure 91; Bekye 202)

Dagaaba do not approach God directly in sacrificial offerings, the latter being considered too great and human sacrifices too meager to be given to him directly. (Bekye 202) The position of the ancestors and the spirits enhances the dignity of the gifts. Prayers before the *Tibe* show a similar belief in the mediatory role of these spiritual agents. For example, the following prayer is said before *Teng-gan*:

> Receive these fowls and the cow and take them to *Saazu-ngmen* (God-of-the-above).

Tibe are agents of communication. In fact, they are said to be *Naangmen na-kyiinbe* (the shepherds of God) with the responsibility of watching over a precise domain of the world. As stated earlier, they are localized in a shrine and act as agents of protection over the people within their jurisdiction. For instance, *Kpime* (ancestors) watch over and protect the family; *Wie* (Lord of the bush) reigns over the vast domain of the wild nature. *Teng-gan* (Earth Spirit/shrine) watches over the village, the cultural sector and human civilization. *Saa* (Spirit of rain) reigns over the celestial phenomena while the *kontome* (Beings of the wild, Spirits of divination) are the wise counselors of human beings. (Bekye 204)

The reference to the *Tibe* as shepherds is significant because, among the Dagaaba, shepherds are usually not owners of the animals they herd. They are mere caretakers. In the case of the *Tibe,* they are mere intermediaries or communication channels between God and human beings. (Bekye 205)

Dreams are also an important channel of religious communication among Dagaaba. It is common belief, among Dagaaba, that God or the ancestors communicate their will to people through dreams. This is particularly the case in deciding whether one should enroll for the *bagre* initiation or not. As Paul Bekye describes, when an elder of a house sees the ancestors (in his dream) appearing to him in great numbers, he gets up in the morning and goes into the *kyaara* (byre) where the carved wooden images of the ancestors are placed in order to pay homage to the *kpime* (ancestors). There he performs a ritual called *kuo-puuru* (spurting of cold water over the ancestral images) to ask for peace. Then he consults a *bag-*

bugre (diviner) to find out why the ancestors have come in his dream. It is usually the diviner who determines the reason the ancestors came to him in his dreams. (Bekye 155–156) When the diviner determines that it is *bagre-ngmen* (deity of the initiates) who has come upon the dreamer, then the latter will consult elders in the family, who will cross-examine the matter with another diviner before asking the dreamer to enroll for the *bagre* initiation rite.

Nature of Human Communication among Dagaaba

In a male-dominated society, communication tends to be horizontal among males and vertical between adult males and females and children, the women being considered "adult children." Females may communicate on a horizontal level among themselves as they usually do on their way to fetch wood or water from the river.

Adult males usually gather together to make decisions bearing on their family or clan. If or when a woman or child is present at such gatherings, they are expected to be silent observers. The model of communication is, therefore, one of dialogue among adult males and submission and obedience to male orders by women and children.

The description of social roles among Dagaaba also indicates another form of communication. There are distinct male roles and female roles in these cultures. For example, men farm, build and repair homes, defend the family or clan in times of war or conflict, etc. while women sow crops on the field, fetch firewood and water, prepare food, bathe the children, sweep the rooms and surroundings. It is unusual for men to perform women's duties, just as it is for women to perform men's duties. Any such performance is ridiculed and the victim made fun of or avoided.

Even without the luxury of writing by means of which modern society easily makes reference to past events, traditional and illiterate Dagaaba were able to remember events, ritual formulas and prayers, moral values, genealogies and the migration stories of their ancestors, which all defined their identity. Obviously, things they remembered were limited to only those events or stories that had a distinctive relation to the individual, family or clan. In the words of Walter J. Ong, protracted orally based thought, even when not in formal verse, tends to be highly rhythmical. Oral cultures also learn to retain information by mnemonic devices. (Ong

34–36) Oral cultures like that of traditional Dagaaba societies learn and communicate by apprenticeship, listening, repeating and participating. These are essential elements in the communication model of these cultures. (Ong 9; Suom-Dery 213)

References

Angsotinge, Gervase. Wisdom of the Ancestors: an Analysis of the Oral Narratives of the Dagaaba of northern Ghana, Ph.D. Dissertation. Los Angeles, CA: University of California Press, 1986.

Bangnikon, Luke D. Wisdom to Guide You: a Book of Dagara Proverbs, Wisdom and Humour with English Translations and Comments, Ghana, 1999.

Bekye, Paul. Divine Revelation and Traditional Religions with Particular Reference to the Dagaaba of West Africa. Rome: Leberit Press, 1991.

Bemile, Sebastian K. The Wisdom which surpasses that of the King: Dagara stories, Brazzaville and Heidelberg: P. Kivouvou Verlag, 1983

Goody, Jack. The Myth of the Bagre. Oxford: Clarendon Press, 1972.

Grindal, Bruce T. Growing up in Two Worlds: Education and Transition among the Sisala of Northern Ghana. New York: Holt, Rinehart and Winston, 1972.

Kpiebaya, Gregory E. "God in Dagaaba Religion and in the Christian Faith." Unpublished STL Dissertation, Lumen Vitae Institute: Universite Catholique de Louvain, 1973.

Kuukure, Edward. The Destiny of Man: Dagaare Beliefs in Dialogue with Christian Eschatology. Frankfurt am Main: Peter Lang, 1985.

Kuuwabong, Dannabang. Naa konga: a Collection of Dagaaba Folktales. Accra: Catholic Press, 1992.

Ong, Walter. Orality and Literacy: the Technologizing of the Word. London & New York: Metheun, 1982.

Suom-Dery, Eugene. The Family as Subject of Moral Education in the African Context: Incarnating Christian Ethics among the Dagara of north-western Ghana. Hamburg, Germany: Verlad Dr. Kovac, 2000.

Tengan, Alexis. Hoe-farming and Social Relations among the Dagara of northwestern Ghana and southwestern Burkina Faso. Frankfurt am Main: Peter Lang, 2000.

Tengan, Edward. The land as Being and Cosmos: the Institution of the Earth Cult among the Sisaala of northwestern Ghana. Frankfurt am Main: Peter Lang, 1991.

Yankson, P. W. K. "Decentralization and traditional authorities" in *A Decade of Decentralization in Ghana: Retrospect and Prospects*, edited by

Thomi, W., Yankson, P. W. K., & Zanu, S. Y. Accra, Ghana: Gold-Tye Ltd, 2000.

Chapter 2
The Cultural Relevance of Myth: A Reader-Response Analysis of the *Bagre* Myth with Reference to the Role and Place of Women in the Dagaaba Society

This chapter was originally published in *Journal of Dagaare Studies*, vol. 5, 2005. It has been revised and is reprinted with permission.

Introduction

In a patriarchal culture like that of the Dagaaba of northwestern Ghana social institutions, folklore and religious rituals can be windows through which one can see, and perhaps, understand the way of life of a people. The *bagre* myth of the Dagaaba is one such window that enables Dagaaba and non-Dagaaba alike to enter into the worldview of this society. Joseph Campbell (1973) affirms this quality of myth when he states:

> Myth is the secret opening through which the inexhaustible energies of the cosmos pour into human cultural manifestation. Religions, philosophies, arts, the social forms of primitive and historic man, prime discoveries in science and technology, the very dreams that blister sleep, boil up from the basic, magic ring of myth. (3)

In a world that has become very conscious of human rights, especially in the area of women's rights, it would be interesting to find out what a traditional myth such as the *bagre* myth of the Dagaaba has to say about women and their place in Dagaaba society. The *bagre* myth is both a traditional myth that seeks to explain some origins, including the origin of life and death in Dagaaba cosmology. It is also a religious rite of passage for people within the Dagaaba society who feel called to this occult institution called the Bagre Association. The myth has been studied and compiled into a book entitled *The Myth of the Bagre* by the English ethnologist, Jack Goody (1972). The section of the *bagre* myth that I have selected to analyze from a reader-response approach gives an insight into women in Dagaaba culture and to some extent, opens areas for conversation about women's rights and their place in Dagaaba society. Some people may argue that the text I have selected brings out little in regard to the place of women in Dagaaba society. However, I believe that whatever little the text has to say in this regard is very significant. A reader-response approach to criticism primarily focuses attention on the reader and the process of reading and not the author or the text. It assumes that reading is a performance, that literature exists when it is read and that meaning is not fixed in a text but a transactional event created by the interaction of the reader and the text (McManus 1998). For Stanley Fish (1972), a reader is a member of an interpretive community. Iser (1978), on the other hand, maintains that a text has gaps that have to be filled by the reader. Hence, for Iser, interpretation "is a dialectic or exchange between text and reader." (Zimmerman 1999, 78)

Like every researcher or analyst, I have my assumptions, presuppositions and biases as I engage this text. First of all, I assume that the text of the *bagre* myth is accurate and authentic. Although I am a Dagao (singular of Dagaaba), I have no first-hand knowledge of the myth and the *bagre* initiation from which the myth originates. The text of the *bagre* myth is the result of an ethnological study by Jack Goody. However, since no Dagaaba scholars or indigenous people with substantial knowledge of the bagre initiation and myth have contradicted the record of Goody, I presume its authenticity. I am also using the English translation of the myth based on my presumption that the translation is accurate. Even as a Dagao, I do not understand the myth when I try to read it in Dagaare.

Secondly, I am reading and analyzing this myth as a Dagao who has been educated in the Western tradition. My analytical tools derive from Western literary theory and rhetorical studies. Therefore, I concede that my educational background in literary theory and rhetoric influence my perception and interpretation of the text.

Thirdly, I am cognizant of the fact that the myth is a text originating from a time different from mine today and that it had a theme: how did the Dagaaba come to know how to procreate? However, my reader-response approach to the text within the context of my historical moment and experience may sometimes lead me to raise questions that may appear to take the text out of context. That is the function of subjectivity that is to be expected in such an analytical approach. Texts are meaningful within the framework of the reader's experience. As Dennis Trevor (1994) observes, meaning is not to be found, so much as created. Meaning is made, or meaning 'happens'... through dialogue with the text. It comes into being in the mysterious process of reading, when text and reader come together. (1)

Finally, I take consolation in knowing that my interpretation of the myth is worth the while because as Joseph Campbell (1973) states, "there is no final system for the interpretation of myths, and there will never be any such thing." (381) My analysis of the myth will not be the first or the last. However, it constitutes a significant contribution to the body of knowledge about Dagaaba and their worldview.

This paper is, therefore, a hermeneutical as well as rhetorical attempt to make the *bagre* myth accessible to Dagaaba and non-Dagaaba of today. It is also an effort to make the myth alive and meaningful to the cultural context of Dagaaba today especially in the area of the role and place of women in Dagaaba society. The paper seeks to establish the practical inseparability between interpretation and language use, i.e., hermeneutics and rhetoric (rhetorical hermeneutics) where hermeneutics is about interpretation and rhetoric is about the production of persuasive discourse and the analysis of a text's effects on an audience. (Mailloux 1997, 379)

From the point of view of Dagaaba culture, the *bagre* myth can truly be said to be a "conduit through which Dagaaba shamans pass down to neophytes an apocryphal vision and perception of Dagaaba spiritual, cultural, and ritual relationship with their seemingly harsh, semi-arid natural environment, which baffles them in its unpredictability, but also, nonetheless, nourishes them." (Dannabang 2004, 1)

Defining Myth

According to Fritz Graf (1993), myth makes a valid statement for a people about the origins of the world, about the gods and their relationship with mortals, in short, about everything on which human existence depends. (3) Graf further asserts that rhetoricians defined myth as a fictitious story that illustrates the truth and that even Plato, who resolutely excluded myths from the realm of truth, believed that, in the realm that could not be reached through dialectical reasoning, myths had at least some expressive power. (4)

Myths are traditional tales that are transmitted from one generation to the other without anyone knowing their origin. They are traditional because their origins are "so far removed in time and space as to be irretrievable." (Graf 1993, 3)

My interest in analyzing the *bagre* myth is to assess its cultural relevance for Dagaaba today, especially in the area of women's role and position in Dagaaba society. Graf explains that the cultural relevance of a myth is quite different from the validity of a philosophical proposition. According to Graf, a proposition is considered valid by anyone who can either prove or disprove its veracity through the use of reason. However, a myth is considered valid only by the community in whose tradition it has taken shape – a community that exists at a particular time and place. Therefore, the cultural relevance of a myth varies with the social context in which it is narrated. (4)

For Levi-Strauss, myth is a mode of communication and can therefore be regarded as a valid window through which to study a culture. Levi-Strauss looks at culture as a series of interwoven communicative systems. In "The Structural Study of Myth," Levi-Strauss (1967) proceeds on the assumption that language and myth are analogous, and employs the instruments of the structural analysis of language to understand myth. (Graf 1993, 44) Roland Barthes (1957), on the other hand, describes myth in his *Mythologies* as a system of signs, like language. (Graf 1993, 53)

According to G. S. Kirk (1970), myths concern us not only for the part they play in all primitive, illiterate, tribal or non-urban cultures, which makes them one of the main objects of anthropological interest; not only for the grip that versions of ancient Greek myths have gained through the centuries on the literary culture of the western nations; but also because of men's endearing insistence on carrying quasi-mythical modes of thought, expression, and communication into a supposedly scientific age. For Kirk, myths do not have a single form, or act according to one single set of rules, either from epoch to epoch or from culture to culture. (1970, 2)

In seeing the prime function of myth as the recording and validating of institutions, and in totally rejecting their speculative aspects, Kirk asserts that Bronislaw Malinowski has succeeded in restricting the vision of far too many anthropologists of the Anglo-American tradition. (Kirk 1970, 6) According to Kirk, myths can possess significance through their structure, which may unconsciously represent structural elements in the society from which they originate or typical behavioristic attitudes of the myth-makers themselves. They may also reflect specific human preoccupations, including those caused by contradictions between instincts, wishes, and the intransigent realities of nature and society. (Kirk, 252)

Kirk asserts further that some myths have a fantasy element. Fantasy, according to Kirk, deals in events that are impossible by real-life standards; but in myths it tends to exceed the mere manipulation of the supernatural and express itself in a strange dislocation of familiar and naturalistic connexions and associations. (Kirk, 268) In fantasy, all the rules of normal action, normal reasoning and normal relationships may be suspended or distorted. The hero suddenly becomes the villain or vice versa; minor actions turn out to have profound consequences; transformations of humans into trees, animals, natural substances or stars require no more explanations, and seem just as arbitrary as, the sudden shifts in time and space. Above all there is no consistency of tone or action, and many problems are left unanswered. (1970, 268-269)

The Myth of the Bagre

Bagre is a performance narrative of origins in which the Dagaaba search for spiritual, cultural, and ritual meanings to their human existence in a harsh, semi-arid natural environment that nourishes them but also baffles them. (Dannabang 2004, 1) It is a celebration with apocryphal potentialities, performed and taught to young men and women, and sometimes to the not so young, during rites of initiation into Dagaaba spiritual, material, and cultural history. (Dannabang 2004, 2) The *bagre* myth is also part of the oral narratives of the Dagaaba. Oral narratives, including myths, constitute a subsystem of Dagaaba culture and are articulated through verbal language. Oral narratives are a very important source of Dagaaba conceptual thought relative to the world, man and society, religion and morality, and, therefore, exercise a strong influence in shaping the thought and life of people. (Suom-Dery 2000, 221) For Angsotinge, myths in Dagaaba oral narrative may be said to belong to *teng-koro yele* (matters of the past). (Angsotinge 1986, 72)

As a specific instance of Dagaaba oral narrative, I want to analyze the mythical discourse between the woman and the boa constrictor in the *Black Bagre* as recorded in Jack Goody's *The Myth of the Bagre* (BB 1934 – 2020).

Reader-Response Analysis of the Black *Bagre* (BB1934-2020; BB1934-1940)

> The boy's mother, when darkness fell, asked the father, "What shall we do to get another child in addition so there'll be two"?

In a patriarchal society where men dominate women in decision making especially with regards to children or child bearing, where inheritance is patri-lineal and children are spoken about with reference to their father not mother why is a woman initiating the discussion about begetting a child? Besides, why is this conversation necessary since they already have one child? How did they get the first boy? According to the *bagre* myth, God gave them the child without teaching them how to beget other children. In fact, God did not teach them to do anything. He "created us, but gave us nothing." (WB 6022-6025) The conversation about getting a child takes place in the night. Is there a reason why this conversation is in the night? Is the night the time for sexual activity? Many Dagaaba associate the night with sexual activity. Since they do not have much of an entertainment besides story telling to do at night, the night is easily regarded as a time for sexual activity.

BB 1941-1950

> The boy's father said to her, "The day after tomorrow I will go to my elder's place, to the spider who will help us to climb up to God's place and get a child."

Is this another Garden of Eden story (Gen. 3) where a man and a woman are put together and they are unable to explore their respective anatomy? With a woman around him does the man not feel any physical attraction to her and a desire to explore her anatomy and vice versa? Is he simply going to refer to God for his needs without venturing into the unknown? Apparently, this is the greatest shortcoming of the man and the woman. God had given them all the basic means of sustaining themselves. It was left to them to make use of the means. (Bekye 1991: 167) They failed to dare.

BB1951-1963

> Day had broken and the boy's mother went to the woods to fetch firewood. She searched till she came to a well-wooded bank. When she got there she saw a creature; a boa constrictor and his mate were playing there. At this the woman broke out laughing.

It is part of the domestic responsibilities of women among the Dagaaba to go to the woods to fetch firewood for domestic use. That is part of what is considered women's duties among the Dagaaba. As McCoy (1988) rightly describes, Dagaaba women regularly "go to the nearest source to fetch water for cooking, bathing, and laundering, and carry it home. Collecting wood for the cooking fire was another difficult and time-consuming chore due to its relative scarcity in the region." (153) Therefore, it is not surprising or out of the ordinary to see the woman in this myth going to the woods to look for firewood. Sometimes, women find snakes in the woods. The immediate reaction of many Dagaaba upon seeing a snake is that they are frightened, they may jump or scream or run to look for an object (such as stone or stick) in order to kill the snake. The reaction may also depend on the distance between the person and the snake. If there is a long distance between the person and the snake, the person may stand still to see what the snake is up to, where it is heading or simply just to decide whether to kill the snake or to let it go. In the myth, the boa and his mate are playing and this causes the woman to laugh. What is the nature of the play? The myth does not say explicitly but we guess it refers to sexual intercourse. By seeing the boa constrictor and its mate in the woods, we can say that the woman was environmentally conscious. She is aware of her environment/surroundings. This is a good quality in a geographic and cultural environment where she can easily be prey to some unsuspecting predator, both human and non-human.

BB1964-1968

> The boa constrictor called the woman to come near and he asked her why she was laughing.

A talking snake! Ordinarily, snakes do not speak. Could this be a fantasy theme in the myth? In Dagaaba folklore and mythology it is not unusual for animals, birds or objects to speak. The fact that the boa and the woman engage in dialogue indicates that they are in close talking distance. The fact of animals speaking with humans is seen in myths across the globe. It is therefore safe to say that this is a universal phenomenon. (Campbell 1973, 7-8, 15; Dannabang 2004: 8)

BB1969-1973

> And she answered, "It's nothing, except the playing gave me pleasure. That's why I laughed."

What is the nature of the play? This is not yet revealed except that it hints at something that has the capacity to give pleasure to the woman.

BB1974-1997

> The boa constrictor said to her, "Do you know this pleasure?" And she replied, "No I don't" and he told her to sit there. She sat quietly. The boa constrictor slept with his mate. They did their work and woman saw and asked him to sleep with her too. He slept with the woman and she got up. When she had done so, she told him his play had pleased her when she had said this the snake told her if she played that game, she'd give birth to many children.

Dagaaba learn by observation and participation. (Dannabang 2004, 5) McCoy states: "It is a safe generalization to say, I believe, that Africans everywhere grasp ideas more readily from seeing them dramatized than they do from listening to them... ." (McCoy 1988, 213) So it makes sense that the boa constrictor asks the woman to watch him play with his mate as a way of showing her what the pleasure is. The woman sits down quietly and watches as the boa sleeps with his mate. Then, the woman asks the boa to sleep with her just as he had done with his mate. This could be seen as learning by apprenticeship. The master performs a job while the apprentice watches and after words the apprentice tries to do the same with the help of the master. Learning on the spot and by apprenticeship is ordinary to Dagaaba. However, it is the woman who takes the initiative to ask the boa to sleep with her. In Dagaaba sexual behavior who initiates, the man or the woman? In this case it is the woman who initiates it. She makes an explicit request. Is this a sign of prostitution, promiscuity, or infidelity? Is there a hint at bestiality? Among the Dagaaba, a man has exclusive sexual rights over the wife, but not the wife over her husband. How is it that this woman so easily gives away her sexuality to someone she doesn't know? Now, while the boa is sleeping with the woman what is the mate of the boa doing? Is she watching as her mate performs this pleasurable thing with a woman? Is the boa's mate happy about what is happening? Nothing is said about the situation or feelings of the boa's mate. Maybe that is not an important consideration in the myth. The message or morale of the myth must reside somewhere else. The woman enjoyed the act and told the boa about the pleasure she had enjoyed. What is the nature of post-sexual dialogue among the Dagaaba? Do they talk about how pleasurable the act was? Who initiates the discussion? Are these the tactics of a prostitute, some flirtatious woman? For the Dagaaba having sex in the bush violates one of the moral prescriptions of *teng-gan* (the earth shrine): "Thou shalt not have sexual intercourse in the bush outside human habitation." (Suom-Dery 2000, 106) Did the woman know about this moral prescription? Did the boa know about it? Probably, the prescription came after man and woman knew how to have sex. Finally, there is a revelation from the boa. If the woman plays that game she would give birth to many children. That is what the woman wanted from her man. Upon hearing this, the woman expresses no joy or excitement that she now knows what to do to get children. She does not thank the boa. She just runs off to her own house. In Dagaaba cosmology and belief, cosmic spirits are sometimes shown as personified objects of the universe which are conceived not just as natural phenomena but as personal beings with spiritual interiority whose visible manifestations are the cosmic objects or natural phenomena. One of the cosmic spirits is *wie* (bush). It is to the bush that the woman goes to fetch firewood. It may be said that by going to the bush the woman is not simply going to the literal bush but to the cosmic spirit (*wie*) where an encounter with the other-world is possible. As Suom-Dery explains, *wie* and the other cosmic spirits are delegates of *Naangmen* who regulate the activity of man while presenting him with the possibility of sustenance and nourishment. (Suom-Dery 2000, 56) The woman learned how to copulate from the boa. According to Dagaaba cosmology animals are lower in rank to human beings. The immediate superiors to human beings who have some intellectual superiority to human beings and who teach or reveal things to human beings are the *kontome* (beings of the wild). They are said to be small in stature inhabiting the hills, rivers and trees. They have exceptional intelligence and comprehensive occult knowledge in comparison to man. *Kontome* are the brain behind the discovery of many aspects of Dagaaba culture – art, music, magic, hunting, medicine, and so on. It is therefore surprising that the snake and not *kontome* is responsible for teaching human beings how to copulate. However, the fact that the woman learned from a lower being in the Dagaaba cosmology shows that Dagaaba are ready to learn from any source: superior or inferior in as far as the information is helpful or beneficial to them.

Did she get any firewood, the primary reason for which she went to the woods? Did she even gather any firewood before she saw the boa and his mate playing? Obviously, the experience is more important than the firewood. When she gets home she tells the man about the game she had seen. Nothing is said about the firewood. She teaches the man the game by showing him how to play it. This is very unusual behavior among the Dagaaba. An adulterous woman must first be ritually cleansed before she can have sexual contact with her man. She may not even prepare food for him while in the state of ritual impurity through adultery. In this situation the woman does not seem to be aware of her ritual impurity or perhaps it doesn't mean anything to her. It is important to note that for Dagaaba, adultery is a serious offense and more so when it is committed in the bush. If not atoned for the traditional belief is that there would be no rain. The culprit must pay a fine to the *teng-gan sob* for the ritual purification. The fine can be in the form of a sheep, a goat, several hens and sometimes cowries. (Bekye 1991, 67) In the case of voluntary consent of a woman the husband has the choice, either to take her back, or else send her back to her parents and request the refund of the bride-wealth (or dowry). With such strict norms surrounding adultery, one wonders why the woman in the *bagre* myth so easily allows herself to be in such an adulterous relationship with the boa. Could the observation of how the boa copulated with his mate not have been sufficient? Did the woman actually have to sleep with the boa in order to know how to do it?

BB1998-2020

> Then the woman got up and ran off to her own house. She reached there and told the man that she'd seen something, a certain game. And the man asked, "What game was that?" She replied, "Wait till I show you." She went to lie down and called the man. He came there and lay down too, and then the woman showed him what to do. And the man enjoyed it too and laughed softly, saying it was true the game was pleasing.

The woman runs off to her house and teaches her man to sleep with her. Apparently, she is very excited. Why is the woman so excited about getting children when in the society she does not have ownership over the children, legally speaking? Among the Dagaaba the woman's worth in marriage is in her capacity to bear children. Barrenness is not favorably looked upon and could be a reason for divorce or for a man to marry another wife. Could that be a reason she is eager to prove her worth, that is, ability to bring forth children? Apparently, she is a good learner because she is able to teach the man how to do it and he enjoys it too. She teaches the man what she did with the boa and he just submits himself to doing what she tells him to do.

The Woman as Heroine/Readiness to Dare

According to Joseph Campbell (1973), a hero is:

> The man or woman who has been able to battle past his personal and local historical limitations to the generally valid, normally human forms. Such a one's visions, ideas, and inspirations come pristine from the primary springs of human life and thought. Hence they are eloquent, not of the present, disintegrating society and psyche, but of the unquenched source through which society is reborn. (19-20)

In the text of this *bagre* myth, the woman is willing to take a risk. She ventures into the woods (separation) where she encounters a stranger and after a brief conversation she is willing to take a chance at learning something new. She is willing to dare, to take a risk (initiation). The venture yields good results in the sense that she learns to copulate and have children, and returns to share the knowledge with her man (return).

> A hero ventures forth from the world of common day into a region of supernatural wonder: fabulous forces are there encountered and a decisive victory is won; the hero comes back from this mysterious adventure with the power to bestow boons on his fellow man. (Campbell 1973, 30)

In this sense the woman is a heroine.

According to the *bagre* myth, *Naangmen* (God) gave man, woman and the child all that they needed to sustain themselves. All that they had to do was to dare, take risks, try something new. But they failed and often returned to God with the help of the spider to seek easy answers to their problems. However, we see that the woman makes a substantial breakthrough in this mentality of lack of initiative and total reliance on God, thereby exposing man to realities and pleasures that were so close to him and yet seemed so distant due to lack of initiative and a daring spirit.

If the *bagre* myth was recited in a religious context, as it usually is, does it have a purpose of rehearsing the origins and past benevolence of a particular deity in order to win his support for the present, or to confirm, maintain the memory of, and provide authority for tribal customs and institutions? If so, are there any significant lessons especially regarding the role and function of women from the myth that the Dagaaba society ignores or has reversed?

If the *bagre* myth is to be regarded as fantasy, we must contend with Kirk that it deals with events that are impossible by real-life standards but tends to exceed the mere manipulation of the supernatural and express itself in a strange dislocation of familiar and naturalistic connexions and associations. Obviously, we can see fantasy themes in the myth especially in the instances of a snake speaking or holding a conversation with a woman and actually having sexual intercourse with the woman.

Mutation of Myth

According to Graf (1993), the reason for the continuous mutation of myth – the motor of the tradition – is its cultural relevance. (3) If conditions change, a myth, if it is to survive, must change with them. In this regard, it is appropriate to ask the question: Does the *bagre* myth change or has it remained the same in spite of significant changes in Dagaaba understanding of God, the world and their social relationships? What is its cultural relevance today? Kuwabong Dannabang has articulated the significance of the *bagre* myth for environmental educators who are concerned with the question of desertification and environmental degradation in that part of West Africa. For the purpose of women's rights and human development in general the *bagre* myth, although it remains intact in terms of content and structure, continues to be significant in as far it remains a point of contact between the irretrievable past and the ever changing present of Dagaaba society and culture capable to revealing messages that have hitherto remained hidden to many Dagaaba. In this particular segment of the *bagre* myth a key revelation is made, namely, that discoveries or advancements in human society come about when people take risks or dare to venture into the unknown. That is the journey of every hero and that will also be a good road toward human and cultural development for Dagaaba.

Conclusion

Myths have a cultural relevance and in the case of the segment of the *bagre* myth I have tried to analyze, we learn that although the woman has abused some Dagaaba moral norms regarding sexuality, she is nonetheless a heroine in the sense that she is willing to leave her familiar environment and journey into the unknown world where she encounters the boa, gains new knowledge about how to copulate and beget children and then returns to share the knowledge with the man. This accomplishment of the woman fulfils the original intention of this segment of the myth which is to answer the question: how did the Dagaaba come to know how to procreate?

References

Angsotinge, Gervase T. Wisdom of the Ancestors: An Analysis of the Oral Narratives of the Dagaaba of Northern Ghana. Los Angeles, CA. Unpublished Ph.D. Dissertation, 1986.

Bekye, Paul K. *Divine Revelation and Traditional Religions with Particular Reference to the Dagaaba of West Africa.* Rome: Leberit Press, 1991.

Bird, Phyllis A. *Missing Persons and Mistaken Identities: Women and Gender in Ancient Israel.* Minneapolis, Minn.: Fortress Press, 1997.

Campbell, Joseph. *The Hero with a Thousand Faces.* Princeton, N.J.: Princeton University Press, 1973.

Fish, Stanley. "Literature in the Reader: Affective Stylistics" in *Self-consuming artifacts.* Berkeley and Los Angeles: University of California Press, 1972.

——. Is there a text in this class? The authority of interpretive communities. Cambridge: Harvard University Press, 1980.

Goody, Jack. *The Myth of the Bagre.* Oxford: Clarendon Press, 1972.

Graf, Fritz. *Greek Mythology: An Introduction.* Translated by Thomas Marier. Baltimore, MD.: John Hopkins University Press, 1993.

Iser, Wolfgang. *The Act of Reading: A Theory of Aesthetic Response.* Baltimore and London: John Hopkins University Press, 1978.

Kirk, G. S. *Myth: its meaning and Functions in Ancient and Other Cultures.* Berkeley and Los Angeles, CA.: University of California Press, 1970.

Kuwabong, Dannabang. "Bagre: A Dagaaba Celebration of Environmental balance Between Humans and Non-Humans," *Journal of Dagaare Studies*, Vol. 4 (1-13), 2004.

Levi-Strauss, Claude. *The Structural Study of Myth and Totemism.* Unknown Binding, 1967.

Mailloux, Steven. "Articulation and Understanding: The Pragmatic Intimacy between Rhetoric and Hermeneutics" in *Rhetoric and Hermeneutics in Our Time: A Short Reader.* Jost Walter and Michael J. Hyde (Eds.). New Haven, CT.: Yale University Press, 1997.

McCoy, Remigius F. *Great Things Happen: A Personal memoir of the First Christian Missionary among the Dagaabas and Sissaalas of Northwest Ghana.* Montreal: The Society of the Missionaries of Africa, 1988.

McManus, Barbara F. 1998. Reader-Response Criticism. <http://www.cnr.edu/home/bmcmanus/readercrit.html, 6/20/2005>

Naaeke, Anthony. "Missionary Catechesis in the Diocese of Wa: Problems and New Approaches," *Journal of Dagaare Studies*, Vol. 3, (22-36), 2003.

The New American Bible with Revised New Testament and Revised Psalms. Nashville, TN.: Thomas Nelson Publishers, 1987.

Trevor, Dennis. *Sarah Laughed: Women's Voices in the Old Testament.* Nashville, Abingdon Press, 1994.

Suom-Dery, Eugene. *Family as Subject of Moral Education in the African Context: Incarnating Christian Ethics among the Dagara of North-western Ghana.* Hamburg: Verlad Dr. Kovac, 2000.

Zimmerman, Joyce Ann. *Liturgy and Hermeneutics.* Collegeville, MN: The Liturgical Press, 1999.

Chapter 3
African Art and Persuasion: The Rhetoric of the *Bera* Among the Dagaaba of Ghana

This chapter was originally published in *Journal of Dagaare Studies*, vol. 6, 2006. It has been revised and is reprinted with permission.

Introduction

This paper contends that the *bera*[1] is a non-discursive visual object acting as an active persuasive interlocutor within the subjective consciousness/conscience of a would-be thief standing face-to-face with an object (such as a mango fruit) that is desired for its capacity to satisfy hunger or pleasure. By describing the *bera* as African art and a persuasive agent meant to protect property from would-be thieves I will explain why a village catechist hangs a *bera* on his mango tree and draw the rhetorical relevance of the *bera* to the Dagaaba. By so doing, I will demonstrate that the *bera* is art, situated rhetoric, and a symbol of cultural moral values among the Dagaaba. This paper will, therefore, contribute to the literary corpus on Dagaaba culture and respond to the appeal of Susan Vogel, who in an article, "Whither African Art? Emerging Scholarship at the End of an Age," (2005, 16) calls for analytical research on African art. This paper will benefit immensely from the research of David T. Doris (2005) whose article, "Symptoms and Strangeness in Yoruba Anti-Aesthetics" describes and analyzes the object the Dagaaba call *bera*. Then, I will draw the rhetorical and pastoral implications of a Dagaaba catechist hanging a *bera* on his mango tree.

Dagaaba believe that any of the spiritual functionaries mentioned: *Tengansob*, *Yidandoo* or *Bagbugre* can solicit and invoke spiritual power on

---

[1] *Bera* is a Dagaare word that means a trap or ambush. It is being used here to refer to an object (art form) serving as a moral voice and guardian over personal property.

the *bera* in order to protect fruits, crops, or any of their possessions. Because the Dagaaba fear the spirits, the spiritual dimension associated with the *bera* constitutes a major reason to be afraid of disregarding it.

African Art: The *Bera*

Art of any kind stimulates human imagination. It is the expression of a creative mind often depicting some aspect of the human condition as it may relate to the terrestrial or the extra-terrestrial, the sacred or the profane.

African art comes in various shapes and forms: music, painting, weaving, pottery, carving, and so on. It is both intuitive and symbolic, often expressing the relationship between human beings and the spiritual world. African art generally conveys a moral lesson. The beauty of African art (aesthetics) goes hand in hand with the content or message it purports to convey. This is seen in the use of the same word to express beauty and moral values in many African societies. For example, the Dagaaba of Ghana use the word, *viel or viele*, to mean both beautiful and good. When Dagaaba say, *o viela* or *o vieleng*, they mean that something is beautiful or it is good. When *o viela or o vieleng* is used to speak about art, the saying indicates that beauty and moral content combine to describe African aesthetics. Benjamin C. Ray concurs that African art generally has a moral basis because it is intended not only to please the eye but also to uphold moral values. Val-Jean Belton further describes the aesthetics of African art (sculptures particularly) as a sum of the characteristics and elements clearly present in all art objects, such as, the resemblance of sculptures to human beings, the luminosity or smoothness of an object's surface, the youthful appearance of sculptures, and the way sculptures portray a reserved or composed demeanor. However, not all African art is pleasing to the African eye.

Some African art is ugly to the African eye and made purposely so because such art is intended to portray the ugly side of human nature, or to frighten people or even to create a distance (emotional or spiritual) between the object and the observer. This is particularly the case with the art works in a diviner's room. In this room, the objects (carvings, clothes, etc.) depicting the spiritual world are not usually beautiful to the African eye but they have the effect of creating an aura of fear, trembling, and reverence. This ugly art or anti-aesthetic may also be said to be true about the *bera*.

In "Symptoms and Strangeness in Yoruba Anti-Aesthetics," Doris describes the aa*le* in Yoruba (called *bera* among the Dagaaba of Ghana) as a "visual guidepost of moral excellence" (2005, 24) which assumes several artistic forms, for example, a dry empty snail shell hung on a tree, a piece of broken calabash with some painting usually with a black substance, an assortment of articles put together in some artistic form, etc.

The objects used to design the *bera* are often obtained from familiar contexts, such as, worn out shoes/sandals, an empty corncob, broken calabash, broom sticks, etc. However, the final artistic form that is designed out of the arrangement of these objects is usually placed at a location that makes it visible to anyone who comes in contact with the property that it is meant to protect. The *bera* is not simply a piece of art; it has a spiritual dimension in the sense that a spirit is invoked upon it to guard property and to punish anyone who steals the property in violation of the cultural moral norms.

The *Bera* as Situated Rhetoric

The communication function of the *bera* is its ability, through visibility to a person, to challenge the person (interlocutor) to examine its symbolic significance and to respond to its moral message. In other words, the *bera* as symbol, "engages the recipient in a visual dialogue" where "seeing and being seen" (Doris 2005, 27) a person is called to the interiority of his/her cultural dictionary in search of the meaning and desired response to the object in front of him/her: "do not steal from here, or this will happen to you," (2005, 26) or "steal, and you will be like this." (2005, 28) As Eugene Suom-Dery (2000) rightly affirms, the "Dagara child is born into a symbolic world and house of symbols" where, by "participating in these symbols he gradually understands them; but often the meaning of the symbols are explained to young people in order to motivate them to live the meaning, values, visions, norms, ideals, expectations and aspirations that they represent and signify." (2000, 229) By learning the meaning and significance of the *bera*, the Dagao/Dagara (singular of Dagaaba) is challenged to respond appropriately to this symbolic moral voice right in front of him/her.

As situated rhetoric, the *bera* involves a summons to moral action. It is an appeal to the conscience. The *bera* summons a person to decide whether to steal or not to steal, to live up to the cultural *mores* it represents or to ignore the cultural *mores*. By growing up and learning the social norms and prescriptive sanctions for good or bad moral action, the Dagao/Dagara knows that the punishment for his/her bad behavior could affect him/her directly or it could be diffused to include his/her relatives or the entire community. All these considerations come to the fore right there and then as the Dagao/Dagara stands in front of the *bera*.

As an appeal to the conscience, there is a psychological dimension to the relationship between the *bera* and the would-be thief (intruder) in the sense that the *bera* touches on the guilt aspect of a person. The intruder experiences feelings of guilt or the lack of guilt depending on a number of situations. First, if the would-be thief (intruder) does not see the *bera*, he/she is normally not affected by the power of the *bera*. Second, if the item being protected by the *bera* is not eaten or used in front of the *bera*, the intruder is not punishable. Third, the intruder can ambush the *bera* by sneaking up to it and either destroying it or plucking it off the item to which it is attached and throwing it away. When this happens the *bera* is rendered ineffective. Fourth, the intruder can seek permission from the *bera* by explaining to it that the intruder is in great need (such as hunger). By asking permission, the intruder avoids being punished by the *bera*. Finally, if the intruder has no intention of selling the items, they are normally not punished by the *bera*.

Although different in many respects, the *bera* may be compared to the modern surveillance camera (Big Brother) which basically says: "I am watching you, do what is right." In other words, the *bera* engages a person in some form of dialogue that leads to moral action.

The *Bera* as Non-Discursive Interlocutor

The interpersonal character of a person vis-à-vis a *bera* may be described by identifying the *bera* as a non-discursive interlocutor or a pregnant cultural narrative ready to give birth. Calvin Schrag (1994) defines narratives as stories "spoken or written" that "comport meanings that are already understood, however nonthematically, by the narrator and the hearer/reader alike." (1994, 214) For Schrag, the meaning of the narrative "resides in the narrative itself as it is informed by the social practices, the intersubjective associations, and the institutional purposes that make up the fabric of our sociohistorical existence." (1994, 214) In the case of the *bera*, the narrator is invisibly present but speaks in and through the object that is visibly present to the observer/interlocutor. Initially, the *bera* appears to the observer as a mere object but as the observer is confronted by it and begins to search through his mind for the meaning of this object, he/she realizes that he/she is face-to-face with an active agent of cultural and moral significance. At this moment, the observer is "interpellated through a communicative act ... made subject before the eyes of centralizing power and expected to respond appropriately, by locating herself (himself) within that gaze – as a suspect." (Doris 2005, 27)

As situated rhetoric the *bera* is significant if it shares the same cultural frame of reference with the observer. Without such a shared frame of reference the *bera* would simply be regarded as a mere object or an ugly piece of art. The shared frame of reference ultimately leads the observer to "activate the efficacy of the objects (*bera*)... by interiorizing their conventional symbolic messages at a moment of critical choice." (2005, 28)

The *bera* is situated within a religio-cultural context where words and objects relate directly with the temporal and the eternal, the terrestrial and the extra-terrestrial, the profane and the sacred. Therefore, because of the combination of creating the *bera* (object) and invoking spiritual power upon it (word), the *bera* is regarded not simply as an object that acts as a scare crow to frighten away would-be thieves but something that actually possesses spiritual power and moral efficacy.

For many Dagaaba, the power of the *bera* to punish or cause sickness and even death to people who disregard its summons, is unquestionable. Dagaaba can point to or give examples of people who disregarded the *bera* and were punished with sickness or some mishap or even death. They can also give examples of people who disregarded the *bera* and stole property without consequence. Nevertheless, the belief in the efficacy of the *bera* is generally acknowledged and feared.

Even though the fear of the *bera* is beginning to fade among Dagaaba Christians and educated people, it must be stated that these people still behave cautiously when confronted with a *bera*. After all, the Bible teaches that "You shall not put the Lord, your God, to the test." (Mt. 4:7)

The *Bera* and Christianity

The work of H. Richard Niebuhr (1956), *Christ and Culture*, can throw light on the relationship between Christianity and Dagaaba culture. According to Niebuhr, Christianity can interact with a culture in different ways. Three of those ways are hostility toward the culture, innocent acceptance of the culture and its values, or discernment and creation of a new culture. Catholic missionaries, especially the Missionaries of Africa, who evangelized the Dagaaba of Ghana, approached the new culture with hostility. The missionaries saw almost every aspect of Dagaaba culture as the work of the devil and, therefore, incompatible with Christianity. (Naaeke 2003, 23) Such a hostile approach calls on Christians "to protect themselves from cultural pollution by maintaining strong Church loyalty as a defense against those invading worlds of superficiality." (Gallagher 1998, 117) Maintaining this distance from pagan culture would give Christians moral authority as they live and witness to the Gospel in their communities.

However, as Christianity grows and takes on an African identity, contemporary African Christians are beginning to engage the Christian message in dialogue with the good values of African culture. This process of discernment is inspired by the Pauline address to the Athenians at the Areopagus (Acts 17). In that speech, Paul re-interprets the pagan practices of the Athenians in the light of the Gospel and discovers that there are some elements of the pagan practices that are indeed the seed for proclaiming the Gospel. In like manner, one could argue that although the *bera* is a pagan symbol, the content of its message (do not steal) is totally consistent with Christian morality and the catechist's use of the *bera* could therefore be said to be an ingenious use of a cultural symbol to teach Christian morality.

Interpreting the Action of the Village Catechist

So why does a village catechist hang a *bera* on his mango tree?
The action of the village catechist is subject to a number of interpretations indicating the inseparable link between rhetoric and interpretation.

First, hanging a *bera* on a mango tree by a village catechist could be seen as an expression of the catechist's dissatisfaction with his Church's failure to instill a strict moral order in Christians such that his mango fruits stand in danger of being stolen if he does not resort to another form of moral deterrence to would-be thieves. This sentiment is expressed by some African critics of Christian morality who accuse Christian morality of "destabilizing the coherent moral order" (Suom-Dery 2000, 28) of African society. For instance, some Dagaaba Christians believe that Christianity has watered down the moral norms of their culture by introducing a God of love and forgiveness to such an extent that some cultural moral norms are wantonly disrespected or disregarded by people without consequence. This dissatisfaction is sometimes manifested in the "superficial juxtaposition of Christianity and African (Dagara) reality" (2000, 460) as may be evidenced by the action of the village catechist.

Secondly, the action of the village catechist may be seen as syncretism. The wikipedia encyclopedia describes syncretism as follows:

> Syncretism is the attempt to reconcile disparate, even opposing, beliefs and to meld practices of various schools of thought. It is especially associated with the attempt to merge and analogize several originally discrete traditions, especially in the theology and mythology of religion, and thus assert an underlying unity.
> Religious syncretism is the blending of two or more religious belief systems into a new system, or the incorporation into a religious tradition of beliefs from unrelated traditions. (Wikipedia)

From this definition, we can infer that syncretism can come about as a result of poor communication between a sender and receiver of a message. The sender may present insufficient or distorted information thereby leaving the recipient to interpret the message within the framework of his (receiver's) cultural experience and misunderstand the meaning of the message in the process of doing so. Therefore, the village catechist himself could have misunderstood or misinterpreted the teaching of the Church within the framework of his culture and consequently his action could trigger off the dissemination of erroneous doctrine and practice that has the potential of degenerating into syncretism. In other words, the action of the village catechist may not have been directly intended to misinform people although it has the potential to do so.

Thirdly, the action of the village catechist could be seen as an attempt at inculturation. Inculturation is an effort to incorporate some good elements of a culture into the Christian message. In this case, the use of the *bera* would be an attempt to inculcate the moral norms of the community through the use of cultural symbolism. After all, the values represented by the *bera* are consistent with Christian morality. This position would be consistent with the Pauline speech at the Areopagus (Acts 17). In this regard, the village catechist's action could be argued as an ingenious use of the Dagaaba cultural *topoi* of fear of the spirits and the impetus to do what is morally right as symbolized by the *bera*. However, the difference between the *bera* used by the village catechist and that used by a non-Christian *yidandoo* or *bagburgre* or *tengansob* is that the catechist does not invoke any spiritual power on the *bera* thereby calling on the spirit to strike any one who steals his property. The catechist only uses the *bera* as a scare crow to any would-be thief.

The danger or flaw of this argument is that the recipient has no way of knowing whether the catechist invoked the power of a spirit upon the *bera* or not and hence the likelihood that the catechist will communicate the wrong message by using the *bera*. Additionally, although inculturation is a positive sign of the growth of Christianity in Africa, this process can mislead people through distortions or inappropriate use of cultural symbols to teach the Christian message especially in a society where the meaning and significance of the *bera* is so closely associated with non-Christian beliefs.

On the other hand, the position of the village catechist as teacher of Catholic doctrine could lower the credibility of the *bera* in the eyes of people. By virtue of his Christian faith and role as catechist, people in the community do not expect the catechist to indulge in occult activity and even if he does they would consider it to be a mere farce. On the other hand, his action could potentially lower his credibility as an agent of catechesis and people would cease to take his message and teaching seriously.

Conclusion

Although the *bera* is just a small part of African art, its rhetorical and cultural significance can be studied from different perspectives. This paper has tried to show the rhetorical function of the *bera* as non-discursive visual object and a summons to moral action. By analyzing the role of the *bera* as situated rhetoric, and non-discursive interlocutor, the paper has shown that a Dagaaba village catechist hangs a *bera* on his mango tree because he deems the *bera* to be a powerful cultural agent that has the capacity to persuade a person not to steal property that does not belong to him/her. The Dagaaba cultural *topoi* (places of argument) of fear and the desire to follow cultural moral values are significant persuasive premises for using the *bera*.

This paper has not been comprehensive in its analysis of the *bera* nor was that its intention. Therefore, the *bera* remains an open cultural symbol and subject for scholarship and analysis especially from the point of view of its relevance to the social, psychological and moral development of the Dagaaba.

References

Angsotinge, Gervase T. Wisdom of the Ancestors: An Analysis of the Oral Narratives of the Dagaaba of Northern Ghana. Unpublished Ph.D. Dissertation. University of California, Los Angeles, 1986.

Aristotle. *The Rhetoric and the Poetics of Aristotle*. Translated by W. Rhys Roberts. New York: McGraw Hill, 1984.

——. *The Nicomachean Ethics*. Translated by J. L. Ackrill, J. O. Urmson, and David Ross. Oxford University Press, 1998.

Belton, Val-Jean. "Africa Art and Aesthetics." (Online source: http://www.yale.org/ynhti/curriculum/units/1998/3/98.03.02.x. html). 5/15/06

Doris, David T. "Symptoms and Strangeness in Yoruba Anti-Aesthetics in African Arts," in *African Arts*, Vol. XXXVIII, Number 4 (24-31), 2005.

Fisher, Walter R. "Narration as a Human Communication Paradigm: The Case of Public Moral Argument," in *Readings in Rhetorical Criticism*, Edited by Carl R. Burgchardt. 2nd Edition. State College, PA.: Strata Publishing, 2000.

Foss, Sonja K. *Rhetorical Criticism: Exploration and Practice*. 2nd Edition. Prospect Heights, Ill.: Waveland Press, 1996.

Gallagher, Michael P. *Clashing Symbols: An Introduction to Faith and Culture*. New York/Mahwah, NJ: Paulist Press, 1998.

Hesselgrave, David J. *Communicating Christ Cross-Culturally: An Introduction to Missionary Communication*. 2nd Edition. Grand Rapids, MI.: Zondervan Publishing House, 1991.

Niebuhr, Richard H. *Christ and Culture*. New York: Harper, 1956.

Ray, Benjamin C. "African Art: Aesthetics and Meaning." Online source: (http://www.lib.virginia.edu/clemens/RMC/exhib/93.ray.aa/Introductio n.html.) 5/15/06.

Schrag, Calvin O. *Philosophical Papers: Betwixt and Between*. New York: State University of New York Press, 1994.

Shorter, Aylward. *African Culture and the Christian Message*. Maryknoll, NY: Orbis Books, 1974.

Suom-Dery, Eugene. *Family as Subject of Moral Education in the African Context: Incarnating Christian Ethics among the Dagara of Northwestern Ghana*. Hamburg: Verlag Dr. Kovac, 2000.

The New American Bible with Revised New Testament and Revised Psalms. The New Catholic Translation. Nashville, Atlanta, London, Vancouver: Catholic Bible Press, 1987.

Vogel, Susan. "Whither African Art? Emerging Scholarship at the End of an Age," in *African Arts*, Vol. XXXVIII, Number 4, 2005.

Wikipedia. http://en.wikipedia.org/wiki/Syncretism

Chapter 4
Toward Intercultural Dialogue: Consolatory Rhetoric in Dagaaba Funeral Rituals and Symbolic Display

The aspiration of many people around the globe is the desire for peace: peace between individuals, between social groups, between political forces in a nation, between states within the international community and between the vast human groups which are distinguished from one another by race, culture, ideology or religion. Writing in 1919, Martin Buber observed that modern man is imprisoned in the shell of his own pride, imprisoned in the shells of society, state, Church, school, economy, public opinion, imprisoned by his own indirectness. Buber appealed to humanity to break through the self-imposed shells (barriers/bridges) and to have contact with other people and cultures. (Moore 1974, 85)

For Pope John Paul II (1983), the aspiration of humanity for peace can become a reality if people, groups, and cultures adopt "an attitude of dialogue." According to John Paul II, "dialogue – true dialogue – is an essential condition for peace." John Paul II asserts that lack of dialogue or false forms of dialogue come about as a result of *a priori* decision to concede nothing or a refusal to listen, or through outright lying or a rigid adherence to ideology. To open the path toward dialogue and peace, this paper will invite the reader to concede that different cultures may do things differently and hence the necessity of listening to difference in cultural narratives, rituals, ideologies, and values. Specifically, the paper will invite the reader to listen to an analysis of Dagaaba funeral rituals and symbolic display as a way of understanding this aspect of Dagaaba culture thereby opening the way for dialogue with Dagaaba. The paper is grounded in the theoretical framework of the philosophy of dialogic communication and the interpretative frame of narrative analysis.

Consolatory Rhetoric

Death is a universal human experience. However, different cultures interpret death, celebrate funerals and seek consolation or deal with grief differently. (Ochs 1993, 119) In general, death "calls for a communal rhetoric in which the community both produces and consumes the consolatory, persuasive messages." In death and through funeral celebrations, "a community persuades and is persuaded." (Ochs, 119) Death brings into existence a rhetorical situation that is replete with its exigencies, audiences, and constraints. Within this rhetorical situation symbolic acts engage audiences in an attempt to bring about multiple changes in those directly and indirectly affected by the death. (Ochs 1993, 21)

Although, rhetorical analysis is usually developed to study discursive language (verbal symbols used in communication), a rhetorical analysis of funeral rituals (often comprising of action and objects) is still possible (Ochs 1993, 120) because in funeral rituals, "symbols – discursive and nondiscursive – are present, presented, and experienced." (Ochs 1993, 121) A closer look at the *paala* (pyre) as a specific aspect of the funeral rituals and symbols of Dagaaba will reveal its role as a rhetoric of display.

The Rhetoric of Display

In the *Rhetorics of Display*, Thomas Benson, series editor of the studies in rhetoric/communication, claims that rhetoric can be disclosed through the lens of display and display through the lens of rhetoric. In this book, Lawrence J. Prelli (2006), grounds the rhetorics of display in the theoretical framework of *epideictic* rhetoric of Aristotle (*Rhetoric* Book 1, Chapter 9), meaning to show forth "on" or "for" as distinguished from the *apodeictic*, meaning to show forth "from" or "by" (as in a demonstrative proof in law court or politics).

Epideictic or ceremonial rhetoric provides an opportunity for a community to celebrate and reinforce values it upholds to be good or bad, inspirational and worthy of emulation, such as, honor, courage, honesty, and hard work. Citing Lawrence W. Rosenfield (1980), Prelli observes that epideictic rhetoric (showing forth; disclosure) entails making manifest or highlighting the fleeting "appearance" of excellence in human experience that otherwise would remain "unnoticed or invisible." In epideictic rhetoric, the orator's task is not to demonstrate or prove virtue but, through verbal ornament and stylistic embellishment, to "set an example" of excellence for listeners or onlookers/participants to behold and take heed of its meaning. (Prelli 2006, 2-4) Hence, by describing the *paala* (pyre) among the Dagaaba as a rhetoric of display, this paper will unveil the virtues of the Dagaaba that are symbolically encapsulated in this cultural non-discursive narrative and call for a collective acknowledgment of the presence of virtue in Dagaaba culture. After all, the ceremonies performed on behalf of the dead affirm the values of the living. (Ochs 1993, 28)

The Philosophy of Dialogic Communication

The importance of dialogue for peace may be grounded in the theoretical framework of the philosophy of dialogic communication. As people of diverse cultures encounter one another in various contexts, efforts to bridge the gap of cultural diversity through dialogue must become an imperative as a way of enhancing communication and understanding between cultures.

From a descriptive point of view, Tullio Maranhao (1990) asserts that dialogue is represented as communication between two individuals (subjects) who share a common background of socio-cultural tradition and immediate interests, who talk to one another by means of a common language, and whose conversation sometimes presupposes and at other times, in addition to that, aims at a consensual understanding of meaning. (5)

Maranhao further observes that from Socrates to Gadamer, although symmetry of participation and goodwill have been regarded as indispensable conditions for the ideal of dialogue, the equality among subjects refers not to their physical, linguistic, psychological, social, cultural, or political characteristics, but to the participation in the process of dialogue itself, which should overshadow all traces of individuation. (Maranhao 1990, 8)

For Martin Buber (1970), man is the being that is capable of entering into relation with the world of things, with other men, and with God. The essential human reality is something that takes place between man and man, between *I* and *Thou* (Buber 1970, 56; Moore 1974, 88). This relationship between I and Thou fulfils the wish of every man to be confirmed as what he is and even as what he can become. Real humanity exists only where this capacity is actualized. (Moore 1974, 89)

Moore further elaborates on Buber's philosophy of dialogue when he states:

> When there is genuine dialogue between partners who have turned to one another in truth, who express themselves without reserve and are free of all semblance, a memorable common fruitfulness which is to be found nowhere else comes into being. (Moore 1974, 92)

Dialogue implies listening to the other and turning toward the other, regarding the other as the very one he is. When the other is reduced to something less than a subject (when a person is reduced to the level of an object) the communication degenerates into an I-It relationship and is therefore, not genuine dialogue.

For Jaspers (cited by Long 1968), an individual's authentic existence may be illuminated by his struggle with others to understand himself and the world in which he is immersed.

> I am I only in relation to another. I grasp myself not as an isolated being but as one who is reciprocally related to another. And the fulfillment of my authentic existence comes about as I stand over against the other without rejecting his I in which my being is mirrored. The awareness of myself is immersed in this reciprocity in which I become myself through the other as he is through me. (Jaspers cited in Long 1968, 97-98)

In their article entitled, "Communication and the ground of dialogue," Kenneth N. Cissna and Rob Anderson identify four relatively distinct but not unrelated conceptions of dialogue that co-exist in contemporary literature. The first, derived from Buber, conceives dialogue as a form of human meeting or relationship. The second, based on the work of conversation analysts, ethnomethodologists and others, uses dialogue to refer to the intricacies of human conversation. A third, derived largely from the work of Mikhail Bakhtin (1986) and his contemporary interpreters, views dialogue primarily as a cultural form of human knowing. A fourth approach to dialogue can be traced to Hans-Georg Gadamer's (1982) philosophy of textual understanding and interpretation. (Anderson et al, 1994, 10) Cissna et al. outlines the following characteristics of dialogue:

immediacy of presence (this suggests both the now and the here dimensions of communication); emergent unanticipated consequences (dialogue is fundamentally improvisational and independent of the will of any participant); recognition of strange otherness (dialogue results when participants refuse to assume that they already know the thoughts, feelings, intentions, or best behaviors of the other); collaborative orientation (dialogue is characterized by high levels of concern for self as well as for the other); vulnerability (dialogue involves risks); mutual implication (in message interpretation we discover something about our communicative partner and ourselves in a unique way); temporal flow (presumes some historical continuity of communicative partners and a sensitivity to the time of the address); genuineness and authenticity: a presumption of honesty until proven otherwise, is offered to the other. (Anderson et. al., 13)

In his *Pedagogy of the Oppressed*, Paulo Freire (1970) describes dialogue as the encounter between men, mediated by the world, in order to name the world. For him, dialogue cannot occur between those who want to name the world and those who do not wish this meaning – between those who deny others the right to speak their word and those whose right to speak has been denied them. Those who have been denied their primordial right to speak their word must first reclaim this right and prevent the continuation of this dehumanizing aggression. If it is in speaking their word that people by naming the world transform it, dialogue imposes itself as the way by which they achieve significance as human beings. Dialogue is thus an existential necessity. (Freire 1999, 69)

For Freire, dialogue cannot exist without humility. The naming of the world through which people constantly re-create that world, cannot be an act of arrogance. Dialogue further requires an intense faith in humankind, faith in their power to make and remake, to create and re-create, faith in their vocation to be more fully human. Faith in people is an *a priori* requirement for dialogue; the dialogical man believes in others even before he meets them face-to-face. Without this faith in people, dialogue is a farce which inevitably degenerates into paternalistic manipulation. (Freire1999, 71-72)

Founding itself upon love, humility, and faith, dialogue becomes a horizontal relationship of which mutual trust between the dialoguers is the logical consequence. For Freire, to "glorify democracy and to silence the people is a farce; to discourse on humanism and to negate people is a lie." Nor yet can dialogue exist without hope. Hope is rooted in men's incompletion, from which they move out in constant search - a search which can be carried out only in communion with others. (Freire 1999, 72)

Finally, true dialogue cannot exist unless the dialoguers engage in critical thinking – thinking which discerns an indivisible solidarity between the world and the people and admits of no dichotomy between them – thinking which perceives reality as process, as transformation, rather than as a static entity – thinking which does not immerse itself in temporality without fear of the risks involved. Only dialogue, which requires critical thinking, is also capable of generating critical thinking. Without dialogue there is no communication, and without communication there can be no true education. (Freire 1999, 73-74)

In his message for the celebration of the Day of Peace (January 1, 1983) Pope John Paul II chose the theme, Dialogue for peace, a challenge for our time. In this message the Pope declared that dialogue presupposes the search for what is true, good and just for every person, for every group and every society. It demands openness and welcome: that each party should explain its thoughts, but should also listen to the explanation of the situation such as the other party describes it, sincerely feels it, with the real problems which are proper to the party, its rights, the injustices of which it is aware, the reasonable solutions which it suggests. (John Paul II 1983)

Toward Intercultural Dialogue

Grounded in the philosophy of dialogic communication, it is reasonable to conclude that peace between people, groups, states and cultures is possible in an environment where a person or people break out of their shell and listen to others as *Thou* not *It*; with an attitude of humility not arrogance; shared experience not a fascination with the self as a measure of justice or virtue; a willingness to be flexible rather than being ideologically fixed and sterile, and a genuine love for truth about the other.

Dagaaba Funeral Rituals and Symbols

Funerals involve a number of performances including rituals and the use of symbols. According to Malidoma Some (1999), ritual offers the opportunity to relieve a tension from which words cannot sufficiently release a person/people. (161)

Funeral rituals and symbols can be described as narrative. Calvin Schrag (1994) defines narratives as stories "spoken or written" that "comport meanings that are already understood, however nonthematically, by the narrator and the hearer/reader alike." (1994, 214) For Schrag, the meaning of the narrative "resides in the narrative itself as it is informed by the social practices, the intersubjective associations, and the institutional purposes that make up the fabric of our sociohistorical existence." (1994, 214) Following this definition of narrative, I argue that Dagaaba funeral rituals and symbols are nondiscursive narratives. As Bell (1992) states, citing Levi-Strauss, what is distinctive about ritual is not what it says or symbolizes, but that first and foremost it does things; ritual is always a matter of "the performance of gestures and the manipulation of objects." (Bell 1992, 111)

Among the Dagaaba, funeral celebrations take place immediately following the death of a person. Death is understood as going home (to the land of the ancestors), meaning that death is actually a passage from one mode of existence to another. (Kuukure 1985, 111) Death involves a journey from the land of the living (earthly life) to the land of the ancestors (hereafter). This belief or conception of death is reflected in the way Dagaaba celebrate funeral rituals. For the Dagaaba, funeral ceremonies demand the greatest participation. Funeral ceremonies involve several actions, symbols and events that function rhetorically.

Rather than duplicate an ethnographic narrative of Dagaaba funeral rituals contained in the works of Kuukure (1985) and Malidoma Some (1993), I intend to engage in a rhetorical analysis of the *paala* (pyre) as a specific instance of a rhetoric of display within the larger context of consolatory rhetoric of the Dagaaba funeral ritual. This analysis will, hopefully, enable non-Dagaaba readers to understand and engage in meaningful and effective dialogue with Dagaaba culture regarding their funeral rites and symbolic displays.

The *Paala* (Pyre or Funeral stand)

The *paala* (funeral stand) is a place where the corpse is displayed for public viewing and mourning. It is usually prepared by the gravediggers at a convenient place near the compound of the deceased. It is made of posts/wood tied together with fiber to make a giant chair with a canopy of cloths for shade[1]. The *paala* faces east if the deceased is male indicating that in life he usually woke up early in the morning, before or as the sun is rising, to go to work on the farm. If the deceased is female the *paala* faces west to indicate that as a hardworking woman she was usually busy at work until the sun sets. In essence, the *paala* is an instance of gendered communication from a nonverbal point of view. The corpse is seated in a dignified position to show honor and dignity of the deceased as well as the respect the living have for the deceased. Around the *paala* material displays of food, animals, clothing, etc. are made to indicate the achievements of the deceased. For a deceased man, a bow is laid across his folded legs and a quiver hangs from his shoulder. The bow and quiver indicate that the man was a hunter and guardian of his household. In an agrarian society like that of the Dagaaba, hunting is regarded as an important duty that men perform in order to feed their families and also to protect them from danger posed by wild animals or an enemy.

As part of the adornments around the deceased male on the *paala* are a public display of horns of animals killed in hunting, farm produce, fowls and animals. These objects show the industry and accomplishments of the deceased as a hunter and a farmer. Money is often strewn around the corpse. The money symbolizes the contribution of the donor toward the success of the long (spiritual) journey that the deceased has begun to the land of the ancestors. Dagaaba believe that on this journey the deceased will have to pay a ferry toll in order to cross the bridge that is believed to connect the land of the living to that of the ancestors.

On a deceased woman's lap will be placed her shrine basket (*tiib-pele*) and in her hand an unscrapped calabash bowl. These objects symbolize her womanhood. Dagaaba women often show hospitality to visitors and strangers by offering them a calabash of water. They may also use a calabash to hold seeds for sowing in the fields. Around the *paala* are placed all other objects that correspond to her role and achievements as a woman – a soup pot, a bathing bowl. (Kuukure 1985, 115)

Two women elders are consecrated to take care of the corpse. They each sit on one side of the corpse with fresh leaves in their hands representing the new life that has started for the dead person. They also use these leaves

---

[1] Today some Dagaaba communities use an arm chair made of wood by carpenters.

to chase flies away from the dead body. These women elders, although they weep discreetly, must be inattentive to what is happening outside the space in which they sit. This is because they are accompanying the dead person, collecting all the grief poured into the space and loading it on the soul of the dead one as it readies itself for the grand departure. (Malidoma 1993, 77)

Interpreting the *Paala* as a Rhetoric of Display

The *paala* is an essential element of the Dagaaba funeral ritual that plays a significant rhetorical function in the process of grief and consolation. In and around the *paala* one finds the entire life and work of a Dagara man or woman displayed in microcosm. The *paala* is a narrative snapshot of the dead person's life celebrating the excellence of Dagaaba cultural values. As family members and the community behold this display of the life of the deceased they are summoned and challenged to witness and take heed of the excellence in the life of the deceased as exemplifying the values of the society and to strive to uphold the virtues by which the deceased lived. According to Malidoma (1993), grief is food for the psyche. It is both individual and collective and the *paala* sets the stage for people to grieve and console one another in the following ways.

Paala as Medium and Harbinger of Grief and Mourning

The *paala* is constructed outdoors as a temporary shelter for the deceased. This location facilitates the participation of family members and the entire community in the funeral rituals. Any Dagao (singular of Dagaaba) who sees the *paala* knows that there is a funeral at the location. The *paala* is designed and adorned in a way that makes it stand out for people to see from near and far. In this way it announces the presence of death and mourning to passers-by.

People know whether the deceased is a man or a woman by taking note of the direction the *paala* faces. If the *paala* faces east, it signals that the deceased is a man, and if it faces west it means that the deceased is a woman.

As a medium announcing the funeral, the *paala* offers an open invitation to everyone to come and participate in the ritual of grief, mourning, and consolation. As a community oriented people, Dagaaba believe that the joys and sorrows of one person or family are the joys and sorrows of everyone in the community and hence the public invitation signaled by the *paala*.

Paala as Site of Public Visitation and Space for Grief and Consolation

By creating a space where the deceased is seated and adorned in ceremonial attire to befit his/her status, Dagaaba prepare the stage for individuals and the community to mourn, grieve, console one another and offer a fitting farewell to the deceased as he/she journeys to the land of the ancestors. Death disrupts the harmony of a community and calls on every community member to attend and assist. (Kuukure 1985, 112) The minimum a person can do to show respect for the dead and sympathy for the deceased family is to show up at the funeral ground, even if for just a short time. (Malidoma 1993, 78) In the space created by the *paala*, people are given an opportunity to grieve publicly.

Paala as Transitional Abode of the Deceased

The *paala* is the new and temporary abode of the deceased that offers the living an opportunity to mourn, celebrate the life of the deceased and prepare to bid him/her farewell for the new life ahead. The manner in which the deceased is displayed on the *paala* can rightly be described in the words of Ochs as a "juxtaposition of opposing elements of symbolic behavior. (Ochs 1993, 48) Although Ochs is describing the Greco-Roman funeral ritual, a number of the following diametrically opposed role reversals in the Greco-Roman funeral are also true for the Dagaaba as they display the dead on the *paala*.

> The corpse is cleared and beautified. The living are dirtied and marred. The corpse is unblemished; the living are disfigured. The corpse is anointed; the living are unwashed. The corpse is draped and covered; the living have ripped and torn raiment. The corpse is displayed at rest; the living are agitated and frenetic. The corpse is touched affectionately; the living receive no reciprocating gestures. The corpse is silent; the living are loud. The corpse is presented to the living as amplified and lifelike a configuration as possible. The reclining, restful posture argues graphically for the tranquility of the death condition. (Ochs 1993, 48)

Between the *paala* and the people there is a space where every emotion is permitted and expected – mourning, dancing, singing, running, etc.

(Malidoma 1993, 77/78) It is a center of attraction and everyone must check in to pay respect to the deceased. Because of its role as the center of attention and activity, people get to know who has come to the funeral and who has not. For example, new arrivals to the funeral must walk past the dead three times in a straight line. At the fourth passing the newcomer must walk toward the dead twice and make an offering as a presentation from himself and his own dead relatives and parents before joining the gathering of mourners. (Malidoma 1993, 79) Because everyone must do the check-in ceremony it is easy to notice who has attended the funeral and who has not. This knowledge is important because reciprocity of respect and sympathy may be dependent upon attendance and participation in this public and communal activity. (Malidoma 80)

In this space, one can also identify the close relatives of the deceased, called *kotuosob*. They are usually "tagged for everyone to recognize."[2] (Malidoma 82) As the *kotuosob* mourns and grieves, people express sympathy and support in various ways. For example, a container or caretaker comes out of the mourners to support the grief-stricken person by loosely holding the tag and ensuring that the *kotuosob* does not get into any harm. The caretaker also receives (monetary) donations from sympathizers on behalf of the *kotuosob*. (Malidoma 83/84)

Paala as Space for Final Farewell

The *paala* is a place in front of which people express their friendship one last time. At the *paala*, friends of the deceased may express sentiments of their friendship and offer gifts (usually animals/birds) to the dead to take along to the land of the ancestors. The gifts express the donor's desire to maintain the friendship with the deceased family. The *paala* is also the locus of *xanu/zanu* (meaning dream or re-enactment), the re-enactment of the life of the deceased by the living (usually friends or colleagues). Through *xanu/zanu* the spirit of the dead must live its life once more in an accelerated fashion before departing to the realm of the ancestors. (Malidoma 85)

[2] The tag is usually strewn from fiber or cloth and tied around the wrist or waist or even hung over the shoulder of the *kotuosob*.

The *paala* is also a place where mourners gather for the final parting ceremony. At this ceremony[3] (while grave diggers/undertakers prepare to take the body of the dead to the grave, xylophones and drums accompany mourning) the physical separation between the living and the dead takes place as mourners mourn and express unformulated grief while the grave diggers take the deceased from the seat to carry him/her to the burial place. At this time, mourners must now let go and allow the deceased to travel to the next abode.

Conclusion

The ceremonies of the dead affirm the values of the society. Values such as, honor, courage, honesty, hard work, and belief in life after death are upheld by Dagaaba and these find expression in the symbolic and ritual celebration in and around the *paala*.

By analyzing the *paala* of the Dagaaba as an example of a rhetoric of display, I have demonstrated that the *paala* has immense rhetorical significance for the Dagaaba. The *paala* is a medium and harbinger of grief and mourning, a site of public visitation and space for grief and consolation; a transitional abode of the deceased, and a space for the final farewell given by the living to the deceased. Although the suasive power of the *paala* on an individual and/or the community cannot be determined with scientific precision, this traditional epideictic event performs an inevitable role that words alone cannot do. As Ochs affirms, "communicative symbols in different and more efficacious registers of action and object languages, are needed." (Ochs 1993: 122) Nonetheless, the ultimate persuasive agent is the individual or the community itself and some comments made by individuals and the community about a funeral and the *paala*, in particular, indicate the persuasive effect of the epideictic experience. For example, some Dagaaba comment (positively or negatively) on the height of the *paala*, the adornments around the *paala* and on the dead body, as well as the attendance at the funeral (who attended, who did not attend, and who is still expected to attend).

Although this paper has not explored every aspect of Dagaaba funeral ceremonies, it is hoped that it will be a stimulus for intercultural dialogue.

---

[3] For families that can afford a coffin, the grave diggers go up the *paala* to take and place the dead body in the coffin and take it away to bury.

As Arnett and Arneson (1999) state, "Dialogic civility is ultimately a reminder that life is best lived with concern for self, other, and sensitive implementation with the historical moment." (304) This paper has, hopefully, been a catalyst and an invitation to open up to Dagaaba culture and engage it in communicative actions that promote understanding and peace between people of different cultures.

References

Aristotle. *The Rhetoric and the Poetics of Aristotle*. Translated by W. Rhys Roberts. New York: McGraw Hill, 1984.

Arnett, Ron C. & Arneson, Pat. *Dialogic Civility in a Cynical Age: Community, Hope, and Interpersonal Relationships*. New York: SUNY, 1999.

Bell, Catherine. *Ritual Theory, Ritual Practice*. New York/Oxford: Oxford University Press, 1992.

Buber, Martin. *I and Thou*. A New translation, with a prologue and notes by Walter Kaufmann. New York: Simon and Shuster, 1970.

Cissna, Kenneth; Rob Anderson & Arnett, R.C. (Eds.). *The Reach of Dialogue: Confirmation, Voice, and Community*. New Jersey: Hampton Press, 1994.

Freire, Paolo. *Pedagogy of the Oppressed*. New York: Continuum, 1970.

——. *Pedagogy of the Oppressed*. 20th Anniversary Edition. Translated by Myra Bergman Ramos. New York: Continuum, 1999.

John Paul II. "Dialogue for peace, a challenge for our time". Pope's message for the celebration of the Day of Peace. Vatican City, 1983.

Kuukure, Edward. *The Destiny of Man: Dagaare Beliefs in Dialogue with Christian Eschatology*. Frankfurt/M. Bern/New York: Peter Lang, 1985.

Long, Thomas E. *Jaspers and Bultmann: A Dialogue between Philosophy and Theology in the Existentialist Tradition*. Duke University Press, 1968.

Malidoma, Patrice Some. *Ritual: Power, Healing, and Community*. New York, NY: Penguin Books, 1993.

——. *The Healing Wisdom of Africa: Finding Life Purpose through Nature, Ritual, and Community*. New York, NY: Penguin Books, 1999.

Maranhao, Tullio (Ed.). *The Interpretation of Dialogue*. Chicago and London: The University of Chicago Press, 1990.

Moore, Donald J. *Martin Buber: Prophet of Religious Secularism*. Philadelphia, PA: The Jewish Publication Society of America, 1974.

Naaeke, Anthony. "The Cultural Relevance of Myth: A Reader-Response Analysis of the Bagre Myth with Reference to the Role and Place of

Women in the Dagaaba Society," in *Journal of Dagaare Studies*, vol. 5, 2005.

Ochs, Donovan J. *Consolatory Rhetoric: Grief, Symbol, and Ritual in the Greco-Roman Era*. Columbia, SC.: University of South Carolina Press, 1993.

Prelli, Lawrence J. (Ed.). *Rhetorics of Display*. Columbia, SC.: University of South Carolina Press, 2006.

Rosenfield, Lawrence W. "The practical celebration of epideictic," in *Rhetoric in Transition: Studies in the Nature and uses of Rhetoric*, ed. Eugene E. White. University Park: Pennsylvania State University Press, 1980.

Schrag, Calvin O. *Philosophical Papers: Betwixt and Between*. New York: State University of New York Press, 1994.

Shorter, Aylward. *African Culture and the Christian Message*. Maryknoll, NY: Orbis Books, 1974.

Chapter 5
Dismantling Fear and Establishing *Ethos*: Missionary Activity as Persuasion

This chapter was originally published in *Journal of Dagaare Studies*, vol. 6, 2006. It has been revised and is reprinted with permission.

Introduction

Why did the Dagaaba of Northwestern Ghana respond so positively to the Catholic evangelization of the Missionaries of Africa? The answer to this question remains open for discussion. For some people, the mass conversion of the Dagaaba to Christianity may be attributed to the "rain miracle." (McCoy 1988, 109-124; Naameh 1986, 179-181) For others, such as, Sean Hawkins (1989), the conversion of the Dagaaba to Christianity may be explained by the "socio-political dimension of the Dagara at the dawn of missionary activity." (Hawkins 1989, 66) For Suom-Dery (2000), the mass conversion of the Dagaaba to Christianity may be said to be "a complex story involving a multiplicity of factors." (Suom-Dery 2000, 40) I tend to agree with Suom-Dery and contend that as a persuasive endeavor, the missionary activity of the Missionaries of Africa successfully employed the rhetorical *topoi* (places of argument or topics) of dismantling fear and establishing *ethos* (credibility or character) with the result that many Dagaaba converted to Christianity.

I will expound my contention by grounding it in the rhetorical theory of Aristotle, Cicero, Quintilian, and Augustine. Then, by analyzing the religio-cultural worldview of the Dagaaba as premises on which persuasive messages may be grounded, I will show that fear was a great burden that bound the Dagaaba to a suffocating *status quo* and that the *ethos* of the missionaries contributed immensely in dismantling this fear thereby opening the way for the conversion of the Dagaaba to Christianity. This paper acknowledges that there are different dialectical variations of the Dagaare language and will be faithful to the dialect that is used by the sources referenced. Otherwise, I'll use the word Dagaaba and Dagaare to refer to the people and language of the people among whom the Missionaries of Africa carried out Catholic evangelization in Northwestern Ghana.

Missionary Activity as Situated Rhetoric

Missionary activity that is geared toward conversion of a person or a group of people from one system of belief or faith to another system of belief or faith can be described as situated rhetoric involving "praxis and judgment" or "moral action." It is an activity that is meant to elicit a person to leave one way of life and embrace another way of life, or one belief for another belief. In order to make this decision or moral choice, "the audience's view of a speaker's moral character is a crucial factor in persuasion." (Johnstone 2005, 222) David Hesselgrave (1991) affirms that although missionaries have been commanded by Christ to preach the Gospel, they cannot command a hearing. They must win a hearing by demonstrating that they are people of integrity, credibility, and goodwill. (1991, 146-147)

In the encyclical *Redemptoris Missio* (The Mission of the Redeemer [RM]) John Paul II (1990) expresses that the identity and goal of missionary activity in the Church has Christian conversion as its aim—a complete and sincere adherence to Christ and his Gospel through faith. John Paul II describes conversion as a gift of God, a work of the Blessed Trinity. It is the Spirit who opens people's hearts so that they can believe in Christ and confess him. (I Cor. 12:3) For John Paul II, conversion gives rise to a dynamic and lifelong process which demands a continual turning away from "life according to the flesh" to "life according to the Spirit." (Rom 8:3-13) John Paul II describes conversion as a means by which a person accepts the saving sovereignty of Christ in a personal way thereby becoming a disciple of Christ (RM 46).

Rhetorically, conversion and Christian life may be described as an investment and a performance. When people invest their resources or talents or life in something that they have come to accept as reliable or dependable they also express the intention to live up to the demands of the investment. In conversion, people declare their investment of faith in Jesus Christ and His Gospel through baptism and the Christian life.

To convert from one faith to another requires persuasion. It is a decision that is freely made for or against a proposition, event or person. The decision to convert to Christianity at the proclamation of the Gospel by missionaries must be an individual affair. This decision has social implications because people live in societies where they share the values of the group. This means that leaving one set of values and embracing another set of values affects a person's interaction with others in the society. As a result, conversion demands a thorough weighing of options by the individual in relation to his society. In this regard, Shorter (1974) observes that "conversion may not always entail the explicit renunciation of previously held social values because it sometimes depends on previous social influences." (75)

The importance of choice as an element of persuasion or conversion, particularly in religious discourse between God and His people, is found in both the Old and New Testaments of the Bible. In the Old Testament, Israel is constantly reminded of her covenant with God and the necessity of choosing between Yahweh and the *baals*. In the New Testament numerous invitations are extended to people to choose between life in the flesh and life in the Spirit, to be for Jesus or against Jesus. (Jn. 6: 22-66; Mt. 26:20ff; Acts 5:1-4; Acts 15) In missionary activity the absence of fear, intimidation or coercion on the part of the convert ennobles conversion. For the Dagaaba, the process of conversion to Christianity was facilitated by the ability of the Missionaries of Africa to dismantle fear that held these people in bondage to the world of the spirits.

Dismantling Fear

Dismantling fear as a prelude to the possibility of choice is very biblical. In both the Old and New Testaments the words, "Do not be afraid" (Lk. 1:11-12; 26-29; 30) become almost a mantra in the communication between God and His people. The words, "Do not be afraid" were also used by John Paul II to usher in his Pontificate during his inaugural homily in 1978 and remained the underlying message of his evangelization in the world. Both biblically and pastorally, dismantling fear is a necessary prelude to the possibility of conversion and mission.

Fear is a universal human emotion. Aristotle defines emotions as "all those feelings that so change men as to affect their judgments, and that are also attended by pain or pleasure. Such are anger, pity, fear and the like, with their opposites." Aristotle defines fear as "a pain or disturbance due to a mental picture of some destructive or painful evil in the future. Of destructive or painful evils only; for there are some evils, e.g. wickedness or stupidity, the prospect of which does not frighten us." (Aristotle 1984, 91; 103-106)

Fear among the Dagaaba was grounded in their belief in or experience of the wickedness of the spirits that interacted with and influenced their terrestrial world so closely. The Dagaaba believe that the gods or spirits are capable of inflicting pain, sickness and even death on the living. (Kuukure 1985, 109) According to Edward Tengan (1991) the most dreaded experience of the Dagaaba is to be under the curse of the rain spirit. (Tengan 1991, 43; Kuukure 1985, 109) Bekye concurs that the rain spirit is particularly feared because of its power to kill by lightening. (Bekye 1991, 183) Another element of the Dagaaba socio-religious experience that brought both blessing and fear to them was the belief in the ancestors. (Bekye 1991, 184) The ancestors, like the spirits, were believed to have power to bless or curse the Dagaaba. Then, there was witchcraft (*suolong/suolu*). The Dagaaba believed that a witch (*suobo)* could take possession of a human being in order to enter a compound of its enemy at night for the purpose of eating his or her soul (McCoy 1988, 64) thereby causing a person to die. The Dagaaba also feared taking risks, especially the risk of abandoning their gods and turning to another God. They were afraid that by departing from the "old ways" they would incur the anger of their ancestors and the punishment of the spirits. (McCoy 1988, 72) Through the process of audience analysis, the Missionaries of Africa realized the crippling role and power of fear among the Dagaaba (McCoy 1988, 63) and began to work tirelessly in order to dismantle this fear and to preach the saving message of Jesus Christ. They did this by establishing a persuasive appeal that Aristotle calls *ethos*.

Establishing *Ethos*

According to Aristotle, *ethos* is the most effective form of proof (Aristotle 1984, 91) in persuasion. *Ethos* could mean a person's actual manner of life (good character or virtue) or a person's ability to appear to be good or virtuous. Aristotle asserts that the orator must appear to possess the qualities of virtue, goodwill, and good sense. (1984, 91) This is very important especially when a controversial topic is under debate. For such topics, *ethos* or the character of the speaker is very important especially when the evidence a speaker presents does not clearly point to a necessary or reasonable conclusion in the minds of the audience. Under such situations, the hearer must rely on the evaluations of the speaker and this requires that the hearer trust the speaker.

Although for Aristotle a speaker's ability to appear to the audience as being trustworthy was a satisfactory criterion of *ethos*, Cicero and Quintilian claim that one must truly be a good person to be a good orator. Cicero does assert that a speaker needs genuine weight of character to call people to action (*De Oratore* 2.333). For example, in Cicero's discussion of Antonius's speech for Norbanus, Antonius is seen to gain credibility by showing himself to be good, virtuous, honorable, and loyal– the characteristics that the audience honored. Cicero's admirer, Quintilian, defines the orator as "a good man skilled in speaking," with the "good man" element being the more important (*Institutio Oratoria* 12.1, 11). The difference between Aristotle on the one hand and Cicero and Quintilian on the other is that for Aristotle the judgment about the credibility or character of the speaker is the responsibility of the audience while for Cicero and Quintilian, irrespective of the audience's perception, the speaker must truly be of good character.

When we turn to Saint Augustine (354-430 C.E.), we find an interest in a rhetoric of persuading audiences to a Christian way of life. According to Burke, Saint Augustine's treatment of rhetoric is at once both narrowed in the sense that it is concerned only with the use of words for one purpose–the teaching of Christianity–widened in the sense that the persuasion it would establish was a doctrine of universal motivation. (Burke 1969, 74-75) Burke sees in Saint Augustine "a sense in which all topics of Christian rhetoric deserve treatment in the grand style, since there is nothing in life that does not somehow bear upon God." (1969, 75)

While saying that a good life on the part of the preacher was the most persuasive ingredient of all in commending Christian doctrine, Saint Augustine placed the power of this doctrine outside and beyond any merely human or natural vessels. A preacher might preach Christian doctrine purely for purposes of self-aggrandizement, or even as a lie, but if he preached it correctly his preaching could do good, because of its intrinsic worth, despite the viciousness of his motives. (Burke 1969, 76) That is to say, "the power of truth transcends the limitations of the personal agent who propounds it." (1969, 76) For Burke, this means that truth can "transcend their virtues also." (1969, 76) In other words, beside the personal character of its agents, the Word of God has intrinsic power to transform and convert a person or people to Christ.

Ethos of the Missionaries of Africa

Hesselgrave (1991) states that "the *ethos* of the speaker may universally be the most important factor in persuasiveness" even though "what constitutes good *ethos* is not necessarily universal." (148) For Hesselgrave, every culture has its value orientations which guide the people in "discovering the ideal *ethos*" of their particular culture." (1991, 148) For Saint Augustine, *ethos* includes the intrinsic character of truth to be persuasive:

> Sometimes when the truth is demonstrated in speaking, an action which pertains to the function of teaching, eloquence is neither brought into play nor is any attention paid to whether the matter or the discourse is pleasing, yet the matter itself is pleasing when it is revealed simply because it is true. Whence many are delighted simply by the exposure and refutation of falsehood. These do not delight because they are falsehoods; but since it is true that they are false, the very language in which this is demonstrated to be true delights. (Saint Augustine 1958, 137)

Following Saint Augustine's exposition on *ethos*, it is reasonable to affirm that the *ethos* of the missionary as an agent of the Word of God (*Logos*, or Wisdom) can be seen on two levels: transcendental (vertical) level and immanent (horizontal) level. On the transcendental level *ethos* is the truth of the Word that is proclaimed. This means that the *Logos* or Divine Wisdom has intrinsic capacity to persuade or to transform people's lives. On an immanent level the *ethos* of missionaries resides in their personal moral attitude or their ability to appear, in the eyes of their would-be converts, to be morally virtuous or both. Although the transcendental meaning of *ethos* must be taken seriously when assessing the persuasive appeal of the missionary evangelization it is equally important to consider the *ethos* of missionaries on an immanent level because, as Saint Augustine asserts,

> when that which is taught must be put into practice and is taught for that reason, the truth of what is said is acknowledged in vain and the eloquence of the discourse pleases in vain unless that which is learned is implemented in action. (1958, 138)

To assess the ability of missionaries to persuade by teaching the truth and putting their message into action, a close consideration of the *ethos* of the missionaries along various lines is necessary.

1. Grounding Mission in a Higher Being

"For we do not preach ourselves but Christ Jesus as Lord." (2 Cor. 4:5)

The missionaries made it clear to the Dagaaba that their mission came from God; "We are messengers of Jesus Christ sent by Him, as he Himself had been sent by His Father." (McCoy 1988, 71) As people who were very religious and who held the office of their religious leaders (diviners) in high esteem, the Dagaaba understood the role and status of a man of God. By invoking God as the source of their mission, missionaries tapped into a powerful cultural premise of authority and respect that could easily lend itself to winning the adherence of the people.

2. Personal Moral Qualities

"The missionary is a guest. He lives in the new culture by the grace of God but also by the forbearance of its citizens." (Hesselgrave 1991, 461)

This statement by Hesselgrave means that personal qualities and interpersonal communication skills are important for the missionary. The personal moral qualities or demeanor of the missionaries was summarized by one of the Dagaaba converts, Alfred Bayo, in the following way:

> They looked so innocent, so kind and delicate in their constitutions. Their speech was so soul-stirring and captivating, it was very hard to part with their presence. Among the reasons for the perseverance in the faith were the personal goodness of the missionaries and their love for the people. Both were expressed in their faces and in their behaviour toward people, that is, their kindly manner and polite way of

talking with them. It was also manifested in their devoted service to the people, especially in their care of the sick. (McCoy 1988, 280)

For the Dagaaba, both male and female missionaries also demonstrated moral uprightness by their fidelity to their celibate vocation. In his memoir, Fr. McCoy recalls that the Dagaaba used to hide in bushes at night hoping to "catch" the priests/brothers in some compromising sexual encounters with the missionary sisters. But after many failed attempts to "catch" them Dagaaba eventually came to believe that these missionaries were truly celibate. (1988, 193)

3. Healing Ministry (McCoy 1988: 167-191)

The healing ministry is closely related to the Gospel ministry. (McCoy 1988, 167) For Dagaaba, as for many Africans, sickness is not merely physical. Healing involves both the body and soul. By proclaiming the Gospel and healing their bodily infirmities (McCoy 1988, 167-191) the missionaries showed love, care and concern for the Dagaaba. This opened the way for persuasion/conversion. When a person sees that someone (speaker) is interested in or cares about his or her bodily and spiritual well being the person often tends to look at the other person (speaker) favorably and will most likely adhere to the speaker's message. After all, actions speak louder than words and as the Apostle James states, "show me your faith and I by my works will show you my faith. (James 2:14-26) By attending to the bodily and spiritual needs, missionaries showed their love and faith.

4. The Rain Miracle (McCoy 1998: 109-230)

Sometime in 1932 there was drought in northwestern Ghana and after several unsuccessful attempts to obtain rain from the gods, the Dagaaba approached the missionaries to solicit the intervention of their God for rain. The prayers of the missionaries yielded good results—rain poured down in torrents and shortly after this, many Dagaaba enrolled in the missionary program of religious instruction—the catechumenate. This event—the rain miracle— has come to be described by some people as the primary reason for the mass conversion of the Dagaaba to Christianity. However, the event does not seem to be unique to the Dagaaba. In the Bible there is a similar situation that called on the Prophet Elijah to summon the prophets of *Baal* to a contest on Mt. Carmel in order to demonstrate whose God was the most powerful (1 Kgs. 18:17-40). The God of Elijah was victorious in the contest leading the Israelites to proclaim Yahweh as their God. In like manner it can be argued that by listening to the supplication of the people and sending rain the God of the missionaries proved to be more powerful and reliable than the gods of the Dagaaba who were unable to give rain to their people when they needed it. Although the rain was seen as an act of God, the event added to the credibility of the missionaries in the eyes of the Dagaaba just as the sending of the fire by Yahweh added to the credibility of Elijah the Prophet in the eyes of the people of Israel.

5. Attitude Toward Witches

"The missionary is an expert in religion" (Hesselgrave 1991: 462).

By virtue of their vocation and mission missionaries are presumed to know a lot about God and the spiritual world. Their faith and teaching about God and the spiritual world must be reflected in their lives. For the Dagaaba the spiritual world involved witchcraft. Witches are feared in African societies because of their perceived ability to "eat the souls" of people. The attitude of the missionaries toward witches or the people accused of witchcraft possession was an act of *ethos*. The Missionaries of Africa did not show any fear of the people who were called witches (*suobo).* The missionaries often told the Dagaaba not to fear their so called witches. The missionaries built hostels near the mission area and brought the so-called *suobo* to live in the hostels. Fr. McCoy testifies that the "Dagaabas were constantly amazed at our lack of fear or concern at the grave danger posed by the proximity of the witches's refuge to the mission house. They came to believe, correctly, that we enjoyed the protection of a Spirit more powerful than the *suobo*. In time, faith in a God all-powerful yet infinitely loving would disperse their continual fear of the spirits." (McCoy 1988, 69)

6. Schools: Creation of Indigenous Agency

The Missionaries of Africa opened schools to educate the Dagaaba. These schools prepared the ground and sowed the seed for indigenous agency. Catechists, for instance, became the first indigenous agents of the Gospel. (McCoy 1988, 94) To some extent, catechists were raised to a pre-eminent position in the villages and could see themselves as close collaborators of the missionaries. Even though the catechists received a salary, the salary was very meager that one could argue, as Donovan does, that such a salary could not to be a significant motivation for the hard and tedious work, even persecution that these catechists often endured. (Donovan 2002, 109-110) Education gave hope to the Dagaaba that they too could one day be like the missionaries in terms of knowledge about God and other areas of human development. By opening schools, missionaries indicated to the people that they did not intend to stay for ever and that the mission would eventually belong to them.

7. Translation

Missionaries were pioneers in introducing the Dagaare alphabet through the work of translating sections of the Bible and some Christian prayers. Two years after the arrival of the missionaries the first Dagaare catechism appeared. For Lamin Sanneh (1990), translation is a fundamental concession to the vernacular, and an inevitable weakening of the forces of unanimity and centralization. According to Sanneh, translation shows that the Gospel is potentially capable of transcending the cultural inhibitions of the translator and taking root in fresh soil (53). Translation also showed that missionaries were interested in the language and culture of their host culture.

8. Saints and Sinners

Without avoiding the critique of over-glorifying the *ethos* of missionary activity it is important to point out that missionaries were not always saints. Some people have criticized missionaries for their ethnocentrism and intransigent attitude toward some elements of the recipient culture. In Africa, for example, the major area of dissatisfaction with missionary activity is marriage. Some Africans and even European missionaries, like Michael Kirwen (1979), have accused missionaries of making pastoral decisions especially in the area of marriage without proper knowledge of the African situation. In fact, Kirwen accuses missionaries of preaching the indissolubility of marriage and turning around to "dissolve" (1979, 15) the marriages of potential converts who were already in polygamous situations. Many Ghanaian Christians, evidenced by the conclusions of the First

National Catholic Pastoral Congress of Ghana (1997, 114) believe that people who were in polygamous relationships prior to hearing the Christian message should have been baptized without having to "divorce" their second or third wives in order to receive baptism. In other respects, missionaries have been accused of foregrounding the superiority of their home culture over the recipient culture thereby creating a barrier in their ability to see the good elements of the recipient culture upon which the Gospel could be sown. Consequently, potential converts were turned away.

In *Christianity Rediscovered*, Vincent Donovan (2002) accused missionaries of not allowing people to respond to the Gospel in their unique way. For him "there must be many responses possible to the Christian message, responses which are filled with promise and meaning, but which have hitherto been neither encouraged nor allowed." (2002, 83)

Conclusion

In his book, *Augustine to Freud: What Theologians and Psychologists Tell Us about Human Nature (and why it matters)*; Kenneth Boa (2004) premises persuasion upon two categories of human needs: religious and physical. Boa identifies the religious needs as the need for forgiveness and grace, need for love and community and need for purpose and hope. He draws the physical needs from Abraham Maslow's hierarchy of needs and corroborates the satisfaction of these physical needs from the Bible.

Based on Boa's assertions, it is safe to say that in the encounter between the Missionaries of Africa and the Dagaaba both categories of needs—religious and physical—seem to have been satisfied to a very great extent. The missionaries made relentless efforts to address the religious and physical needs of the people. Missionaries worked hard to dispel fear. They were agents of forgiveness for those who were falsely accused of witchcraft. They gave hope to the sick, women and those oppressed by the evil spirits. They intervened through prayers by securing rain during a period of severe drought. They showed love and communion by being constantly in close proximity with the people, eating their food, playing with them, visiting them in their homes, and teaching them in the schools. Above all, they pointed them to a God who loves, forgives and provides for His people. In sum, the missionaries shared *ethos*, that is, "the quality of our dwelling-together" with the Dagaaba. (Johnstone 2005, 223)

Rhetorically, the psycho-religious as well as the cultural premises of persuasion were adequately fulfilled by the missionaries. The missionaries' personal virtue and works could be sufficient grounds for persuasion and conversion. However, we can say along with Augustine that in spite of the immanent *ethos* of the Missionaries of Africa, the Word of God itself constituted the true *ethos* (transcendental *ethos*) with potential to effect conversion. Irrespective of the moral virtue of its agent, the Word of God effects what it purports to accomplish because, like rain, it must wet the ground and like a double edged sword, it cuts through the bone right unto the marrow.

Cognizant that conversion is sometimes slow and that the Word of God has intrinsic *ethos*, it is proper to end on the note of hope that even those who have not positively responded to the seed of the Word of God sown by missionaries are in some way reaping the fruits of the saving work of Jesus Christ.

References

Aristotle. *The Rhetoric and the Poetics of Aristotle.* Translated by W. Rhys Roberts. New York: McGraw Hill, 1954/1984.

Bekye, Paul K. *Divine Revelation and Traditional religions with Particular Reference to the Dagaaba of West Africa.* Rome: Leberit Press, 1991.

Boa, Kenneth. *Augustine to Freud: What Theologians and Psychologists tell Us about Human Nature (and why it matters).* Nashville, TN.: Broadman & Holman Publishers, 2004.

Burke, Kenneth. A *Rhetoric of Motives.* Berkeley, CA: University of California Press, 1969.

Cicero. *De Oratore.* Loeb Classical Library Vol. 348, Translated by E. W. Sutton & H. Rackham. Cambridge, MA: Harvard UP, 1996.

——. *De Inventione.* Paperback Edition, Kessinger Publishing, 2004.

Donovan, Vincent J. *Christianity Rediscovered.* Maryknoll, NY. Orbis Books, 2002.

Hawkins, Sean. "A Study of Law and Marriage among the LoDagaa of Northern Ghana, 1907-1984." Ph.D. Dissertation, St. John's College, The University of Cambridge, 1989.

Hesselgrave, David J. *Communicating Christ Cross-Culturally: An Introduction to Missionary Communication.* 2nd Edition. Grand Rapids, MI.: Zondervan Publishing House, 1991.

Hyde, Michael J. (Ed.). *The Ethos of Rhetoric.* Columbia, SC.: University of South Carolina Press, 2004.

John Paul II. *Redemptoris Missio* (The Mission of the Redeemer). Boston, MA: Pauline Books & Media, 1990.

Johnstone, Christopher L. Book Review. *Quarterly Journal of Speech,* Vol. 91, No. 2. 222-227. Routeledge: Taylor and Francis Group, 2005.

Kirwen, Michael. *African Widows: An Empirical Study of the Problems of Adapting Western Christian Teachings on Marriage to the Leviratic Customs for the Care of Widows in Four Rural African Societies.* Maryknoll, NY: Orbis Books, 1979.

Kuukure, Edward. *The Destiny of Man: Dagaare Beliefs in Dialogue with Christian Eschatology.* New York, Frankfurt am Maim: Peter Lang, 1985.

McCoy, Remigius F. *Great Things Happen. A Personal Memoir of the First Christian Missionary among the Dagaabas and Sissalas of northwest Ghana.* Montreal: The Society of Missionaries of Africa, 1988.

Naameh, Philip. "The Christianization of the Dagara within the Horizon of the West European Experience." Ph.D. Dissertation. Germany: Westfalische Wilhelms Universitat, 1986.

Quintilian. *Institutio Oratoria.* Translated by H. E. Butler. Loeb Classical Library. Cambridge, MA.: Harvard UP, 1920.

Saint Augustine. *On Christian Doctrine.* Translated by D. W. Robertson, Jr. New Jersey: Prentice-Hall, 1958.

Sanneh, Lamin. *Translating the Message: The Missionary Impact on Culture.* Maryknoll, NY: Orbis Books, 1990.

Schutrumpf. "Non-Logical Means of Persuasion in Aristotle's *Rhetoric* and Cicero's *De Oratore*," in *Peripathetic Rhetoric after Aristotle.* Edited by W.W. Fortenabaugh and David C. Mirhady. New Brunswick.: Transaction Publishers, 1994.

Shorter, Aylward. *African Culture and the Christian Message.* Maryknoll, NY: Orbis Books, 1974.

Suom-Dery, Eugene. *Family as Subject of Moral Education in the African Context: Incarnating Christian Ethics among the Dagara of Northwestern Ghana.* Hamburg: Verlad Dr. Kovac, 2000.

Tengan, Edward B. *The land as Being and Cosmos, the Institution of the Earth-cult among the Sisala of Northwestern Ghana.* Frankfurt am Main: Peter Lang, 1991.

The New American Bible with Revised New Testament and Revised Psalms. The New Catholic Translation. Nashville, Atlanta, London, Vancouver: Catholic Bible Press, 1987.

Weaver, Richard. *The Ethics of Rhetoric.* Chicago: Regnery, 1953.

Chapter 6
Breaking the Silence on Domestic Violence: Communication for Development in Northwestern Ghana

This chapter was originally published in *Gender and Behaviour*, vol. 4, no. 2. It has been revised and is reprinted with permission.

Introduction

In her article entitled "The Intolerable Status Quo: Violence against Women and Girls" (1997) Charlotte Bunch writes that "violence against women and girls is the most pervasive violation of human rights in the world" that affects development in both subtle and blatant ways. (1997, 41) Bunch asserts that violence against women is so "deeply embedded in cultures around the world that it is almost invisible." (1997, 41) This observation resonates well with the published research of Rosemary Ofei-Aboagye, "Altering the Strands of the Fabric: A Preliminary Look at Domestic Violence in Ghana." (SIGNS, vol. 19. No, 4 1994, 924-938) In this essay, Ofei-Aboagye restricts domestic violence to "wife-beating", such as, a slap, push, or use of a weapon. Although domestic violence is much broader than wife-beating the Ghanaian experience is that in most cases it is the husband who beats his wife, although the reverse is also true.

This paper will analyze the phenomenon of domestic violence using the restricted definition (wife-beating) offered by Ofei-Aboagye and contextualize the analysis within a peripheral society called the Dagaaba who reside in Northwestern Ghana. By doing so the paper will add voice to the struggle of women throughout the world for the recognition of their fundamental human rights, especially the right against discrimination and violence of any kind pursuant to the Convention on the Elimination of All Forms of Discrimination Against Women (CEDAW) adopted by the

United Nations General Assembly on December 18, 1979 and the Declaration on the Elimination of Violence Against Women (1993)[1]. Secondly, the paper will establish the fact that although domestic violence communicates power and control by the perpetrator over the victim, the phenomenon can be eliminated through the use of communication. This will happen when victims dare to speak out.

In order to accomplish these goals the paper will endeavor to answer the fundamental questions that are of interest to development communication, namely, why do people do what they do? What are the barriers to change and at what costs will people change? Then, through a qualitative review of the available literature on domestic violence and the cultural philosophy of the Dagaaba of Northwestern Ghana in particular, the paper will use development communication theory to expound on the thesis that communicating to break the silence about domestic violence is essential for development in Northwestern Ghana.

The Reality of Domestic Violence

There are many definitions of domestic violence. Some people define domestic violence as rape, beating and insults faced by women at one end, husbands not getting their meals on time, wives not giving their husbands a massage, etc. (Narayan et al. 2000, 120) However, domestic violence is generally described as "a crime of power and control committed mainly by men against women, a crime in which the perpetrator does not consult the victim's wishes and from which he will not let her escape." (Jones 1994, 126) Domestic violence often involves physical beating, such as, a slap, push, use of a weapon. Sometimes, it is verbal, involving severe criticism, intimidation, threats, humiliation, and/or isolation.

In Ghana, domestic violence is often referred to simply as the beating of a wife by her husband or vice versa. It also involves the excessive beating of children by their parents, where excessive means inflicting severe injury on the child. According to the published research on domestic violence conducted in Tabe Ere in the Lawra district of Northwestern Ghana some Dagaaba men acknowledged the fact of domestic violence or wife-beating when they stated that:

---

[1] Cited by Muthien et al in "When Rights are wronged: Gender-based violence and human rights in Africa."

> there is some violence against the women ... because some husbands beat up their wives when they refuse to obey what the man says. Some also beat up their wives when they do not readily give in to sex. Consequently, rape is another form of violence committed against women. (Narayan et al. 2000, 120)

Domestic violence often occurs behind closed doors (Bunch 1997, 42) but often within earshot or eyeshot of children and family relations. For some feminist scholars, like bell hooks (as in original text), the use of the word "domestic" to describe the brutality against women by men or vice versa sanitizes the crime and suggests that the violence "emerges in an intimate context that is private and somehow less threatening, less brutal, than the violence that takes place outside the home." (hooks 2000, 62) In the Ghanaian social context of the extended family system, family members (immediate nuclear family and the extended family including grandparents, uncles, etc.) often live together in large compounds. This living arrangement is supposed to serve as a support system for members who may be suffering in any way. The living arrangement also sustains the cultural philosophy that, as much as possible, family issues should be discussed and solved within the family in order to avoid throwing away the baby with the bath water. In other words, when the problem of domestic violence occurs, many families among the Dagaaba prefer to deal with the issue within the family without allowing it to be known by people who are not from the family. If only this family living arrangement of the Dagaaba were effectively used to resolve family conflict and address the concerns of family members who become victims of domestic violence the incidence of this phenomenon would have been reduced to the minimum or dealt with to the satisfaction of the victims (often women). Unfortunately, things do not often work out that easily. In many instances, family members in many Dagaaba households tend to blame the woman who is beaten rather than her husband, or she is made to blame herself for the violence inflicted upon her or yet still, she is afraid to report the violence to anyone outside the family. When a woman among the Dagaaba can no longer tolerate the beating by her husband and cannot get the support from the extended family members she often returns to her biological family. When this happens the man's family would usually go and ask for forgiveness and plead for her to return to her husband. At such occasions members of her husband's family would assure the family of the woman that when she returns to her husband the violence will not happen again.

Why Wife-beating?

Why do men beat their wives in Northwestern Ghana and often without consequence? The answer to this question can be as varied as the instances of domestic violence. For example, some people say that "women are hit because lunch is not ready when the husband gets home" (Narayan 2000, 122) or it's "because of unemployment and poverty that most men in this community beat their wives. We have no money to look after them." (Narayan et al, 123) Others blame alcohol and drug abuse or women's dependence on their husbands for social and economic support (Narayan et al, 123). According to the published research of Ofei-Aboagye[2] the following reasons were given by Ghanaian women to explain why husbands beat their wives.

> He would beat me whenever he was drunk, When I confronted him with evidence of his sleeping with another woman, When I asked him for chop-money (housekeeping money), When I refused to have sex, There was no particular reason, Because I was pregnant, He accused me of sleeping with another man, Because my cooking was not to his taste, He said I was rude in public, I had insulted his mother, I spent too much money. (Ofei-Aboagye 1994, 929)

Notwithstanding these reasons, one may adduce a philosophical grounding of wife-beating in Ghana, but particularly among the Dagaaba in Northwestern Ghana, to a cultural philosophy of male superiority over the female. In support of this claim, Narayan et al (2000) affirm that in "many social contexts, domestic violence is supported by social norms" (Narayan et al., 123) such as a "cultural ideology which promotes the primacy of man over the woman." (Suom-Dery 2000, 199) Esther Appiah, Commanding Officer of Women and Juvenile Unit of the Ghana Police Service agrees with this philosophy when she remarked:

---

[2] Ofei-Aboagye interviewed 50 women in Accra, the capital city of Ghana in 1994. Some people may say that sample population is small. However, it is significant because the experiences of this sample is representative of the majority of women and I can also testify to the accuracy of these statements from my personal experience.

> There is too much superiority complex among their (referring to women) male counterparts. They (men) feel women cannot think on their own; they think women are part of their property. Some Ghanaian men even think they should decide what a woman should do.

These affirmations tend to support the claim that domestic violence or wife-beating is grounded in the cultural philosophy that subordinates women to men with the unfortunate outcome that women in many Ghanaian societies have often been ill-treated by men.

By analyzing the cultural philosophy of the Dagaaba about man and woman described by Suom-Dery (2000, 196-201) and the place of the bride price in Dagaaba marriage described by Kuukure (1985), a certain irony appears to be obvious in the sense that domestic violence seems to be tolerated or even normalized by the Dagaaba notwithstanding the moral and social functions the bride price is supposed to play in the Dagaaba society.

In *The Destiny of Man: Dagaare Beliefs in Dialogue with Christian Eschatology*, Kuukure (1985) states that the bride price is exchanged and accepted as a sign and guarantee that the woman will be well taken care of by her husband and new family. Kuukure further states that besides being a token of gratitude to the family of the bride for taking care of her and for allowing her to be a wife to a man in the new family (her husband), the bride price elevates the value attached to the bride as a person and as a wife. (1985, 29) If Dagaaba exchange the bride price for these noble reasons, why do they appear to condone the beating of women by their husbands? Beating and injuring a woman devalues the woman as a partner in marriage, takes away her beauty and diminishes her dignity as a human person. According to Narayan et al. the bride price can become a reason for wife-beating in some societies because "of issues around how much dowry was promised or paid or the sense of owning a woman after 'buying' her through the bride price." (Narayan, 123) Could it be the case that Dagaaba men beat their wife/wives because they think that the bride price gives them ownership over the woman and so they can treat her in any way they want? For Goody (1962) the answer is in the affirmative because according to the Dagaaba, a woman "is considered a possession of her husband's family, paid for with cattle and / or other prestations so that she can be of economic and other benefits to her husband." (Goody 1962, 79)

Bishop Kpiebaya agrees when he writes this about the position of the Dagaaba women:

> A woman is considered to be only a grown up child. She doesn't have equal rights with the man in many respects. This mentality has given rise to all sorts of adverse customs and practices against women. For instance, in marriage the woman is considered to be the property of the husband and his clan but the man is by no means her property.... This attitude of treating women as property and as a hired hand is strengthened by the payment of the bride-price for a wife.... The inferior position of the wife also legitimizes the practice of the man taking multiple wives or indulging in conjugal infidelity. A man has exclusive sexual rights over his wife, but not the wife over the husband. (Kpiebaya 1979, 17-19; cited in Hawkins 2002, 284)

Secondly, Suom-Dery makes the following observation regarding the role and place of men and women in Dagaaba society.

> A close study of Dagaaba social life reveals that the position and place of men and women in their society are determined by the very fundamental principle on which modernists and Christians sensitive to women issues base their claims and demands: equal dignity of man and woman. (Suom-Dery 2000, 196)

If Suom-Dery's claim is true, one wonders why this society has sometimes ill-treated women as Suom-Dery himself affirms when he writes:

> Not seldom, the principle of complementarity for harmony often degenerates into suppressive superiority complex on the part of men, and into condescending inferiority complex on the part of some women. The Dagara society was and still is an imperfect society like all societies. (2000, 200)

Perfect society or not, wife-beating is an affront to the dignity of a woman (every woman) and a violation of the Convention on the Elimination of All Forms of Discrimination Against Women (CEDAW) and the Declaration on the Elimination of Violence Against Women (1993) to which Ghana is a signatory.

Another contradiction between the Dagaaba philosophy and the reality of their social life regarding the place and role of men and women is found in their saying, "*a nisaale dung no?*" [Is a human person an animal?]. (Suom-Dery 2000, 197) This saying or rhetorical question is meant, ostensibly, to affirm the dignity of every human person as deserving of respect and not to be reduced to the level of an animal. Suom-Dery explains that the saying expresses "a fundamental principle that governs the relationships between individuals in the family and the community at large." (2000, 197) However, given the incidence of wife-beating among the Dagaaba, it is reasonable to argue that wife-beating is a counter witness to the cultural philosophy described by Suom-Dery. Wife-beating simply reduces a woman to the level of an object—like an animal—and not a subject worthy of respect and dignity.

Furthermore, Suom-Dery argues that the Dagaaba perception of a woman is two-fold. Sometimes, the Dagaaba regard the woman as a "Nobody", inferior to men, having no rights or voice in the family and society—a grown up child. On the other hand, Dagaaba regard woman as "Everything," the backbone of the family and society. (2000, 200) This contradictory perception of woman may also explain the reality of domestic violence among the Dagaaba depending on which cultural lens on "woman" one looks through. If one looks through the distorted cultural lens that accentuates the role of woman as "Nobody" then wife-beating makes sense. However, such a skewed and distorted cultural philosophy that relegates a woman to the level of an object must not be allowed to prevail in the face of international and universal human rights declarations and conventions. On the other hand, if one looks at "woman" through the lens of her being "Everything"—house builder (*yir miere*), the backbone of the family (*yir kpeng*), the educator (*wulwule*), the peace-maker (*yel-maale*)—characteristics the Dagaaba consider to be desired in an ideal woman (*pog yuor, pog menga*) [Suom-Dery 2000, 201] then wife-beating makes no sense. After all, why would a person want to do harm to such an important human resource in the family or community? In general, wife beating does not only violate a woman's right to dignity and respect, it is a major threat to development.

Domestic Violence and Development

Domestic violence is a major threat to development in many ways.

1. Domestic violence is a major threat to health.

Domestic violence inflicts physical, psychological and economic pain on an individual and society. The time and costs involved in treating the physical injuries or psychological trauma inflicted by domestic violence could have been appropriately used to develop some aspect of domestic and community project to improve the quality of life of the people. According to Bunch, violence debilitates women and girls physically, psychologically and socially, sometimes with lifelong results. Besides, women's aspirations and achievements are powerfully inhibited, not just by the injuries of physical attacks but by the implicit threat of male violence. (Bunch 1997, 42-43)

2. Domestic violence is a threat to social development

Domestic violence is a key component of social problems, including street children, child labor and prostitution. (Eyiah, Ghanaweb.com, 8/13/2003) Research and daily experience of working with street children by Catholic Action for Street Children (CAS) and Street Girls AID (SAID) strongly indicate that the problem of street children is a major social problem requiring public funding that could have been used for other areas of national or community development (Shanahan 2001), such as, education, vocational training or the provision of social infrastructure in the country.

3. Domestic violence is a threat to self-esteem

By subjecting women to physical abuse and without a social structure that endeavors to stop this practice, women can be made to believe that they are actually inferior to men and that they deserve the abuse. This can affect their self-image and perception of men in general. When a person has low self-esteem he/she is unlikely to value the importance of his/her ideas and consequently will refrain from sharing ideas or perspectives that could trigger development. This can lead to a dependency situation in which women will look up to men for everything instead of trusting in their capacity to deal with situations themselves. In order to overcome these threats to development, communication is essential.

Development Communication

Different scholars[3] define development and development communication in different ways. Some scholars view development in terms of modernization which is "based on neoclassical economic theory

[3] I refer to the perspectives of Agunga, 1997; Berlo, 1960; Kruijer, 1987; Lasswell, 1948; Bella, 2003; Mozammel & Schecter, 2005; Taniguchi, 1992.

and promoting and supporting capitalistic economic development." (Melkote 2001, 130) Others who see development from a critical perspective "challenge the economic and cultural expansionism and imperialism of modernization" while arguing for "a political and economic restructuring to produce a more even distribution of rewards and resources between and within societies." (Melkote, 130) A third perspective on development, according to Melkote, is the liberation or monastic perspective. This outlook on development derives from liberation theology "which prioritizes personal and communal liberation from oppression as the keys to self-reliance, which is seen as the goal of development." (Melkote 130) A fourth perspective to development identified by Melkote has to do with empowerment, a concept which in turn introduces the concepts of power and control in development theory and practice. (Melkote 130) Within the purview of all these perspectives to development, Melkote observes that "development communication scholars and practitioners still tend to be split between those who view communication as an organizational delivery system and those who view communication more broadly, as inseparable from culture and from all facets of social change." (Melkote 130) Anand and Amartyak (1996) define development in terms of "dealing with and overcoming issues of the high incidence of premature mortality, poor health, malnutrition, illiteracy, poverty, insecurity and other forms of deprivation." (Anand & Amartyak 1996, 3)

No matter which perspective of development one takes, the communication function of development is to be a tool. Communication is an essential handmaid of development in the sense that communication offers effective channels or strategies which practitioners of development communication use to promote development in any of its forms. Therefore, development communication or communication for development may be described as an effort to put communication strategies at the service of development. In this vein, the role of development communication to the problem of domestic violence or wife-beating in Northwestern Ghana will be to facilitate change in the cultural philosophy and experience of the nature of the relationship between men and women by offering communication strategies to all those who have a stake in the problem.

Breaking the Silence on Domestic Violence: Individual Initiative and Institutional Support

As a social "construct of power," (Bunch 1997, 44) domestic violence or wife-beating can be changed. The change may not take place overnight but must begin somewhere with someone or group of people taking the first step by daring to speak out.

In Ghana, the inspiration or impetus to assert their human rights and to demand respect from men comes from many sources including women groups, such as, the National Women's Council, the 31st December Women's Movement, and the Christian Mothers' Association. These groups have begun to educate women on their rights and dignity through meetings, radio and television programs, workshops, etc. As women groups continue to support women initiatives toward development, there is an urgent need for institutional backing within the country. However, there is no clear cut legislation on domestic violence in Ghana. President J. A. Kufuor has created a cabinet position for women and children and the police have established the women and juvenile unit (WAJU) to provide victims of domestic abuse with support. However, WAJU is not yet available in all regions of Ghana.

There is a bill in parliament on domestic violence in Ghana which is under discussion. This bill broadly defines domestic violence to include any threats or acts of physical, emotional or verbal harm that take place within a previous or existing domestic relationship. It defines domestic relationship as an association among a group of people at the same place permanently. Examples of people in domestic relationship include married couple, people who are engaged and living together, have or are expecting a child and people who are related to one another including parents.

Notwithstanding the delay in arriving at a national policy on domestic violence some form of action has to be taken in order to prevent this crime from continuing to occur. The action required must be grounded in the two pillars of development (Anand & Amartyak 1996, 27), namely, individual initiative and institutional support.

1. Individual Initiative[4]

The individual has the responsibility for his/her own development with the support of the institutions around him/her. Some ways that an individual takes initiative to develop him/herself are the following:

- Awareness of one's situation and the possibilities for progress. Women of Northwestern Ghana and indeed, throughout Ghana are already conscious of the subservient and undignified way in which they are treated by men and their culture. This consciousness has been facilitated through education, women groups, such as, the National Women's Council, the 31st December Women's Movement, and the Christian Mothers' Association. The desire of women to liberate themselves from the indignity of domestic violence is also seen when a woman returns to her father's house in order to resist the cruelty of her abusive husband. However, more initiative can come about through further education, newspapers, traveling, listening to the radio or television, or through interpersonal encounters with other people, etc.
- Dialogue: awareness should lead to dialogue with other people (including family members and other authority figures), asserting one's rights (without being aggressive). This means that women must speak directly to their husbands on the level of equality and partnership or on the basis of subjects (I–You and not I–It) as Buber explains. (Buber 1970, 54-56)
- Forming or aligning with existing groups that share your vision for change/development. I have already mentioned a number of women's groups that inspire hope and champion the cause of women rights in Ghana. Women should be encouraged to join these groups and make their voices heard.
- Education: education opens doors to development. For example, to avoid being misled, an uneducated person may enroll in a literacy program in order to gain the basics of reading and writing. Or, a school drop-out could decide to go back to a vocational school to learn some vocational skills, etc. Education can also help

---

[4] This section is inspired by Paolo Friere's *Pedagogy of the Oppressed*, 1973 and Martin Buber's *I and Thou*, 1970.

people to learn different ways of dealing with their differences without resorting to domestic violence.

- Employment: with employment comes income and this is a major source of empowerment. When a person earns income from his/her job the person is less likely to be dependent on others and this can significantly reduce the incidence of domestic violence. This is especially important given the fact that women are often afraid to speak out against domestic violence because of the financial consequences of doing so.

2. Institutional Support

Institutional support must come from all institutions that have a stake in promoting human rights. These institutions must include the family, chieftaincy, churches or places of worship, the local and national government, as well as international bodies that defend human rights.

- The Family: Nuclear and Extended

In Northwestern Ghana, for example, the family extends beyond the nuclear family (father, mother and children) to the extended family (uncles, aunts, grandparents, clan members, etc.). The Dagaaba family (*yir*) was a major source of support for individuals and must continue to play this role even as the society undergoes change due to urbanization, education and the introduction of the money economy. The institutional support from the family may come in the form of parents refusing to have their daughters genitally mutilated, or family members saying positive things about their sister- or daughter-in-law, or by women speaking out about their experiences of violence to other people within or outside the family who are capable of assisting them to overcome the problems.

- Groups/Associations

Groups, such as, the National Council for Women and Development, the 31st December Women's Movement, The Christian Mothers' Association and many others are great avenues of support for women as they seek to develop their self-esteem and assert their rights in society. These groups are also avenues for women to develop and improve upon their leadership and communication skills that are all necessary for development. These groups can organize people to work for great causes that lead to development.

- National and local authority

The role of national and local authorities, such as, the president of a country or parliamentarians, or district assembly members, is to come out with policies and ensure the proper execution of policies for the benefit of citizens. Their most fundamental role in civic society has to be the desire for justice for all the citizens they serve.

- Religious Institutions/leaders

In many respects, Christian and Muslim religions and leaders have replaced the traditional role of the *teng-daana* or *tengan-sob* (custodian of the earth/land) among the Dagaaba. Before the advent of Christianity and Islam, the *tengansob* used to perform religious as well as legal functions. He offered sacrifice on behalf of his people and settled disputes that arose between or among his people. These roles have largely been taken over by the Christian and Muslim leaders. As a source of institutional support for development, religious leaders must create environments where people can go to have their religious and human needs met, have their conflicts resolved and even to have someone to listen to their problems.

- NGOs and International Organizations

Non-governmental organizations at local, national or international levels play an important role in development. They empower many segments of the population in Northwestern Ghana by providing micro-credits, grants, donations, counseling services and expert advice to individuals and groups. To accomplish their role effectively, representatives of NGOs should respect the local culture and endeavor to work in collaboration with the communities they serve.

The available channels of communication through which messages about domestic violence can be disseminated are face-to-face communication (on the interpersonal and group level including homilies in Churches and mosques), the radio (through Radio Upper West, Radio Progress [both in Wa] and FEED Radio [in Nandom]), and television. A myriad of traditional and modern communication formats can be used to convey messages about domestic violence and the importance of speaking out against this phenomenon. Some of these formats include educational songs against domestic violence, dramatic displays, books, newspaper reports, campaigns, flyers, posters, etc.

Conclusion

This paper has tried to expound upon the thesis that breaking the silence on domestic violence is important for development in Northwestern Ghana. Through an analytical review of available literature, the paper has established that among other factors domestic violence is rooted in a cultural philosophy of the superiority of men over women. However, as a social construct, this cultural philosophy can be challenged and overturned when women and all those who have a stake in promoting human rights speak out against domestic violence and seek ways to eliminate its continuous occurrence in Northwestern Ghana.

When the full potential of every human resource base in Northwestern Ghana is put to use, development will become a reality. By eliminating domestic violence, its victims, especially women, will regain their self-esteem and dignity. Then, the unfortunate consequences of domestic violence, such as, withdrawal, lack of communication, angry outbursts, aggressive behavior and low self-esteem will be removed thereby empowering everyone to contribute his/her share toward development. In addition, time and money lost in seeking medical attention and paying medical bills will be saved or properly used for other development projects of families and communities, such as, paying school fees for children and procuring food for the family. But above all, the absence of domestic violence will lead to true love, care and peace in families with the capacity to reduce the incidence of rural-urban migration by young people and the high incidence of street children in the nation's cities.

Finally, the paper has certainly not been comprehensive in dealing with the issue of domestic violence in Northwestern Ghana, nor was that its intention. This means that the subject remains open for further research, especially for empirical research, on the effects of individual initiative and institutional support that enable women to speak out against domestic violence. Specifically, it would be important to pursue empirical research on the role education and employment of women play on reducing the incidence of domestic violence.

References

Agunga, Robert. *Developing the Third World: A Communication Approach.* Commack, NY: Nova Science Publishers, 1997.

Anand, Sudhir & Amartyak, Sen. *Sustainable Human Development: Concepts and Priorities.* UNDP/ODS. New York, 1996.

Bekye, Paul K. *Divine Revelation and Traditional Religions with Particular Reference to the Dagaaba of West Africa.* Rome: Leberit Press, 1991.

Berlo, David K. *The Process of Communication: An Introduction to Theory and Practice.* San Francisco: Rinchart Press, 1960.

Buber, Martin. *I and Thou.* New York: Simon & Shuster, 1970.

Bunch, Charlotte. "The Intolerable Status Quo: Violence against Women and Girls." in *The Progress of Nations*: 41-45, 1997.

Eyiah, Joe Kinsley. Ghanaweb.com, 8/13/2003.

Freire, Paolo. *Pedagogy of the Oppressed.* New York, NY: The Seabury Press, 1973.

Hawkins, Sean. *Writing and Colonialism in Northern Ghana: The Encounter between the LoDagaa and "the World on Paper.* Toronto: University of Toronto Press, 2002.

hooks, bell. *Feminism is for Everybody: Passionate Politics.* Cambridge, MA: South End Press, 2000.

Jones, A. *Next Time She'll be Dead: Battering and How to Stop it.* Boston: Beacon, 1994.

Kessey, Charles Boady. *Participatory Implementation: The Gender Dimension in the Implementation of Community-level Projects in Ghana.* Helsinki University Printing House, 2004.

Kpiebaya, Bishop Gregory E. 1979. "Living the Christian Life Today," in *That They May Have Light: An Account of the Activities of the Church in North-West Ghana 1929-1979*, edited by Father V. Gregoire. Wa Catholic Press, 1979.

Kruijer, Gerald J. *Development through Liberation: Third World Problems and Solutions.* Translated by Arnold Pomerans. Atlantic Highlands, NJ: Humanities Press International, 1987.

Kuukure, Edward. *The Destiny of Man: Dagaare Beliefs in Dialogue with Christian Eschatology.* Frankfurt/M: Peter Lang, 1985.

Lasswell. H.D. "The Structure and Function of Communication in Society." in L. Bryson(Ed.). *The Communication of Ideas*. New York: Harper and Brothers, 1948.

Melkote, Srinivas R. & Steeves, Leslie H. *Communication for Development in the Third World: Theory and Practice for Empowerment.* 2nd Edition. New Delhi: Sage Publications, 2001.

Mody, Bella. (Ed). *International and Development Communication: A 21st Century Perspective*. Thousand Oaks: Sage Publications, 2003.

Mozammel, Masud & Schecter, Gailia. *Strategic Communication for Community Driven Development: A Practical Guide for Project managers and Communication Practitioners*. The World Bank, Washington, DC, 2005.

Muthien, Bernedette & Combrinck, Helene. *When Rights are wronged; Gender-based Violence & Human Rights in Africa*. Publication forthcoming in *Transnational Transgressions: African Women, Struggle and Transformation in Global Perspectives*. M. Bahati Kuumba and Monica Wjite (Eds). No facts of publication.

Narayan, Deepa, et al. *Voices of the Poor: Crying Out for Change*. New York: Oxford University Press, 2000.

Ofei-Aboagye, Rosemary. "Altering the Strands of the Fabric: A Preliminary Look at Domestic Violence in Ghana." *SIGNS*, vol. 19. No. 4, 924-938, 1994.

Shanahan, Patrick. "The Alternative Africa: Street Children in Ghana." CYC-online, Issue 25, February, 2001.

Snyder, Leslie B. "Development Communication Campaigns," in *International and Development Communication: A 21st Century Perspective*. Edited by Bella Mody. Thousand Oaks, CA: Sage Publications, 2003.

Suom-Dery, Eugene. *Family as Subject of Moral Education in the African Context: Incarnating Christian Ethics among the Dagara of North-western Ghana*. Hamburg, Germany: Verlag Dr. Kovac, 2000.

Taniguchi, Makoto. "Participatory Development: A Key Element in Development Strategies for the 1990s" in *Change: Threat or Opportunity for Human Progress?* Edited by Uner Kirdar. United Nations, New York, 1992.

Online Newspaper Sources

—The Haggling Over Domestic Violence Continues

<http://www.peacewomen.org/news/Ghana/May05/Violence.html> (8/6/2006)

—News from Africa: Struggling to Flush out Domestic Violence <http://www.newsfromafrica.org/newsfromafrica/articles/art_809.html> (8/6/2006)

—Public Agenda–Accra, December 1, 2003. "Sixteen Days of Activism against Gender Violence." <http://www.peacewomen.org/news/Ghana/Dec03/activism.html> (8/6/2006)

—Ghana Launches Campaign Against Domestic Violence <http://www.feminist.org/news/newsbyte/uswirestory.asp?id=9770> (8/6/2006)

—"Causes of wife and women abuses in matrilineal and patrilineal families in Ghana." <http://www.ghanaweb.com/GhanaHomePage/NewsArchive/artikel.php?ID=108760

Chapter 7
Liberating the 'Mistress' in Africa: The Prophetic Role of Development Communication

This chapter was originally published in *Gender and Behaviour*, vol. 5, no. 2. It has been revised and is reprinted with permission.

Introduction

In the book, *Voices of the Poor Crying out for Change*, Narayan et al (2000) assert that poverty or bad quality of life has multiple, interlocking dimensions that combine to create and sustain powerlessness, a lack of freedom of choice and action. But this must not be the case if Africa and Africans are to develop. The development of the poor in Africa has to involve the spiritual dimension of the liberation of women (referred to in the title as 'mistress'), children and men. For development to become a reality every person in the society must be free to make choices, to act without fear of some inhibiting customs or traditions and to take responsibility for the consequences of their actions. However, the spiritual dimension of development communication has not always been given its rightful place in the literature of development communication. Some scholars, particularly H. Leslie Steeves, (2001 and 2003), have tried to address this lapse in the literature and my paper will be an additional voice that affirms the invaluable role of spiritual liberation of the human person, particularly women, in development communication. By drawing upon theoretical concepts of dialogue and prophetic imagination developed by Martin Buber (1970) and Paolo Freire (1973) on the one hand and Walter Brueggueman (2001) on the other, this paper, through a qualitative analysis of available data and research, will show the invaluable role that prophetic imagination has to play in the liberation of women in the development agenda of Africa.

By using the word 'mistress' to refer to women, the paper will draw from the insights of John Stuart Mill's essay, *The Subjection of Women* (1869). The word 'mistress' is used in order to express a number of sentiments about women in Africa and their role in the development agenda of Africa. Some African societies may rightly understand the word 'mistress' to refer to a concubine or girlfriend outside marriage. However, the word 'mistress' is used by J. S. Mill as a title for women—"the mistress of every home" (Mill 85)—to refer to an old fashioned title for the lady of the house, especially one who is head of the household. I use the word mistress to convey two main sentiments. First of all, to show that development communication must endeavor to liberate both the concrete woman as a human person (self-determining subject), and secondly, to restore a more positive meaning of the word mistress by expressing the conviction that the liberation of women must entail the elimination of the utilitarian cultural mentality about the place and role of women in society in which the woman's role is restricted to performing household chores and giving pleasure to men.

In *The Subjection of Women*, Mill develops the following thesis that I intend to further develop and apply to women in Africa.

> The principle which regulates the existing social relations between the two sexes—the legal subordination of one sex to the other—is wrong in itself, and now one of the chief hindrances to human improvement; and that it ought to be replaced by a principle of perfect equality, admitting no power or privilege on the one side, nor disability on the other. (Mill: 7)

In many African societies, the subjection of women to men is usually cultural (Suom-Dery 2000, 200) and not necessarily legal. Whether cultural or legal, the subjection of any of the sexes to the other inhibits development and must be eliminated as a matter of the human right of a person—every person without exception. It is also an infraction of the human rights treaties that guarantee what are considered to be the fundamental rights[1] of every human person, especially women.

Inspired by the arguments of J. S. Mill and in solidarity with the quest of women throughout the world, but particularly in Africa, for the recognition of their fundamental human rights, this paper contends that development communication has an invaluable prophetic role to play in liberating the 'mistress' in Africa as an imperative for development in the continent. The paper follows the definition of liberation offered by Gerald J. Kruijer in *Development through Liberation: Third World Problems and Solutions* (1987) – the elimination of those conditions that constrict life. (Kruijer 1) Liberation must entail "a process that involves a leap forward of consciousness, organization and activity, and that leads to a society based on liberty, fraternity and equality" (Kruijer 3) which ultimately leads to self-fulfillment. (Kruijer 37)

The words "liberating" and "prophetic" are worthy of note. By using the word "liberating" instead of "liberation", I want to focus on the ongoing nature of women's struggle for the recognition of their fundamental human rights. Using the word liberation in the title of this paper would have implied that the act of liberation is accomplished once and for all. Needless to say, the struggle for the recognition and respect of human rights of every person must remain a continual struggle, often requiring prophetic voices to call society to its moral responsibilities toward the weak, the voiceless and those who are socially marginalized. This paper identifies the role of development communication and the development communicator as prophetic, where "prophet" is used as a metaphor to refer to the unending conscience of the society.

By identifying some situations of the "mistress" in Africa, the paper will show the "sufferings, immoralities, evil of all sorts, produced in innumerable cases by the subjection of ... women" and why such situations "are far too terrible to be overlooked" (Mill 85) not only because they are a brutal violation of human rights but also because of their consequences for development in Africa.

---

[1] See the UN Universal Declaration of Human Rights, December 10, 1948; Convention on the Elimination of all forms of discrimination against women (CEDAW), December 18, 1978; Elimination of violence against women, 1993.

I must point out that although the subject of women liberation is not new in Africa or at the international level (Baserup 1970; Huston 1979; Charlton 1984) I agree with Kruijer that "what matters is the need to bear in mind at all times the importance of using the most rigorous approach possible towards a phenomenon that is far from new but persists, namely the oppression of the majority of mankind." (Kruijer 6) This paper will use the development communication approach to address the subjection of the "mistress" in Africa calling for an ongoing process of liberation as a prophetic function.

The Situation of the 'Mistress' in Africa

There are innumerable descriptions of the situation of African women in books, journal and popular articles, television and radio reports, travel narratives and so on. From these sources, the situation of women in Africa is often described as deplorable and destitute. Women in Africa are often portrayed as the beasts of burden and depicted in movies or art work carrying babies on the back while at the same time balancing wood or water jars on the head. The cover page of Maria Rosa Cutrufelli's (1983) book, *Women of Africa: Roots of Oppression*, clearly illustrates this depiction of the African woman. The picture shows five African women each carrying either a clay pot or a bucket (of water, most likely) with the lady in front also carrying a baby on her back. African women are often depicted or portrayed as victims of lack of representation in politics, domestic violence, workplace inequality, sexual harassment, poverty, education, forced marriage, polygamy, and genital mutilation. For instance, in the foreword of *Third World Women Speak Out*, Arvonne Fraser states that "women's traditional economic roles confine them to tasks which, however critical to society ... are not remunerated in cash and reinforce their low status in increasingly monetized economies." (Huston 1979) In this book, the women of Kenya are reported as saying,

> We still have little legal freedom. We are dominated by males through a lack of legislation that would protect us from unjust divorce, polygamy, or unfair inheritance practices and abandonment. (Huston 1979, 8-9)

Christine Obbo (1980) also asserts that African women are culturally expected to cultivate the land and feed their children (8) although in many instances they have no legal rights over the farm produce and in some societies they have no right to inherit the property (land) of the husband when he dies.

In general, therefore, the situation of the African woman is one of subjection to man, a situation many African women have often resisted or forced by tradition to accept.

Resisting the *Status Quo*

African women have not always accepted their traditional roles defined by their societies. There is evidence that many women in Africa have often resisted the *status quo*. The motivation for resistance may be attributed to a confluence of influences, such as, Christian missionary activity, migration, education, employment opportunities, and through individual agency. In *The Untold Story: The war through the Eyes of Somali Women*, edited by Judith Gardner and Judy El Bushra (2004) it is asserted that conflict sometimes creates occasions for women to transform their lives and redefine their gender roles as men go to war leaving women as heads of households and to take on traditional male roles. For instance, in the article, "African Women Ready to Lead" Mutume (2006) states that the experience of war or armed conflict has had the paradoxical result of "opening up opportunities for women to change gender relations and to enter into positions of leadership." (Mutume 9) Mutume further asserts that in some conflicts women fight alongside men thereby asserting their equality and winning some bargaining power in post-conflict settlements. (Mutume 9) For some women, the motivation to break ties with traditional expectations may come in the form of a devastating divorce. This was the experience of one Somali woman for whom the civil war became a lesson that "a woman can live on her own." She came to this conclusion (during the war) when she learned that her husband had decided to divorce her, leaving her and her year-old daughter to fend for themselves. (Gardner and Bushra 51) Through these myriad of influences, African women are stepping outside of their traditional responsibilities to earn a living and help bring food to the table through petty trade, vending, casual labor, factory employment, etc. (Narayan et al. 111)

One instance of resistance to the situation of subjugation of African women may be summarized in the formulations of the charter of Women of South Africa called "The Women's Charter, 1954" outlined in Cheryl Walker's book (1982), *Women and Resistance in South Africa*. In the preamble of this charter, the women of South Africa state:

> We, the women of South Africa, wives and mothers, working women and housewives ... hereby declare our aim of striving for the removal of all laws, regulations, conventions and customs that discriminate against us as women, and that deprive us in any way of our inherent right to the advantages, responsibilities and opportunities that society offers to any one section of the population." (Walker 279)

In the formulation of the charter, the women of South Africa do not only acknowledge the fact of discrimination against them simply because they are women, they also assume active agency in seeking redress of this situation. This charter is quite representative of the struggle by African women through time and space to reverse the situation of their cultural subjection to men. (Obbo 1980, 4-5; Huston 1979, 8-9) Another example of the dissatisfaction of women with their traditional roles is described in *Writing and Colonialism in Northern Ghana: The Encounter between the LoDagaa and "the World on Paper", 1892-1991*. In this book Sean Hawkins (2002) enumerates several cases depicting women in Northern Ghana during the colonial and post-colonial periods (1892-1991) who sought to liberate themselves from the shackles of traditional marriage systems. In the cases that Hawkins compiled from the district courts in Northern Ghana, it is evident that those women who resisted forced marriage or polygamy or abuse by the husband often sought justice in the colonial courts or from the missionaries. (Hawkins, 234-252) In his memoir, *Great Things Happen*, Missionary Priest Remigius McCoy (1988) also describes other instances of Dagaaba women resisting their expected traditional roles by escaping to the missionaries for refuge.

In an effort to further the course of liberation for African women, the work of J. S. Mill, *The Subjection of Women* (86-90) may help inspire motivation and action that leads to advocacy on behalf of women's liberation. In this book, J.S. Mill opines that mankind would be better off treating women as equals than subjecting them to men. Mill offers a number of arguments in favor of women liberation. First of all, Mill argues that liberating women from their subjection enables a relationship between men and women that is regulated by justice and not injustice. Secondly, by liberating women from domestic or household chores and allowing them to join the work force outside the home there is doubling mental faculties for the higher service of humanity. Thirdly, Mill argues that by liberating women their opinion would possess a more beneficial influence upon the general mass of human belief and sentiment. Fourthly, liberating women ensures that men and women generously give of themselves to each other thereby promoting a happy life. But above all, Mill argues, is the unspeakable gain in private happiness to the liberated half of the species.

To these reasons I add the urgent need for every hand and talent—of men as well as women—in the development agenda of Africa. In this regard the role of development communication is very important to liberating women in Africa.

Development Communication

Development is increasingly being defined in terms of improving the environment in which poor people live either by providing them with services that will improve their situation or by giving them opportunities to engage in activities that will improve upon their situation. (Charlton 1984, 45) Different scholars[2] define development and development communication in different ways. Some scholars view development in terms of modernization which is "based on neoclassical economic theory and promoting and supporting capitalistic economic development." (Melkote 2001, 130) Others who see development from a critical perspective "challenge the economic and cultural expansionism and imperialism of modernization" while arguing for "a political and economic restructuring to produce a more even distribution of rewards and resources between and within societies." (Melkote 130) A third perspective on development, according to Melkote, is the liberation or monastic perspective. This outlook on development derives from liberation theology "which prioritizes personal and communal liberation from oppression as the keys to self-reliance, which is seen as the goal of development." (Melkote 130) A fourth perspective to development identified by Melkote has to do with empowerment, a concept which in turn introduces the concepts of power and control in development theory and practice.

---

[2] I refer to the perspectives of Agunga, 1997; Berlo, 1960; Kruijer, 1987; Lasswell, 1948; Bella, 2003; Mozammel & Schecter, 2005; Taniguchi, 1992.

(Melkote 130) Within the purview of all these perspectives to development, Melkote observes that "development communication scholars and practitioners still tend to be split between those who view communication as an organizational delivery system and those who view communication more broadly, as inseparable from culture and from all facets of social change." (Melkote 130) Anand and Amartyak (1996) define development in terms of "dealing with and overcoming issues of the high incidence of premature mortality, poor health, malnutrition, illiteracy, poverty, insecurity and other forms of deprivation." (Anand & Amartyak 1996: 3)

No matter which perspective of development one takes, the communication function of development is to be a tool. Communication is an essential handmaid of development in the sense that communication offers effective channels or strategies which practitioners of development communication use to promote development in any of its forms. Therefore, development communication or communication for development may be described as an effort to put communication strategies at the service of development. In this vein, I contend that the role of development communication[3] in liberating women in Africa has to be prophetic. By using prophet as a metaphor, I intend to discuss development communication from the wider perspective that involves the cultural, political, economic and religious liberation of people.

Development Communication and the Prophetic Imagination

Although Moses "did not engage in social action," (Brueggemann 2001, 21) we can learn from his prophetic imagination and draw some parallels or implications for development communication and the role of a development communicator. My contention is that the role of development communication in liberating women in Africa must be prophetic. According to Walter Brueggemann (2001), the "task of prophetic ministry is to nurture, nourish, and evoke a consciousness and perception alternative to the consciousness and perception of the dominant culture around us." (Brueggemann 3) Just like prophetic ministry, the task of development communication is to facilitate change by raising the consciousness of people and communities about their present

[3] Here I must acknowledge the contribution of reputable scholars and practitioners of development communication such as Mozammel & Gailia (2005).

situation and the possibilities for an alternative reality. By performing his/her function as facilitator of change, the development communicator should be able to criticize the *status quo* as well as "energize persons and communities" (Brueggemann 3) by offering hope for a better future. The *status quo* regarding the relations between men and women in many African societies is grounded in a cultural philosophy or *pathos* that subjects women to men. Many women have been socialized to accept these traditions even though some women realize that some traditions inhibit their ability to develop their full human potential. Yet, as social constructs, cultural traditions can be changed just as "the imperial religion and imperial politics" (Brueggemann 7) of Egypt crumbled through the prophetic role of Moses. The impetus for change must come about through the prophetic voice of the development communicator acting in response to the cry of African women for liberation. This is because "the narrative of liberation begins with the grieving complaint of Israel [Ex 2:23-25]." (Brueggemann 11) In the case of African women, the cry for liberation has already been sounded through individual and /or group acts of resistance to cultural domination by men. Although the development communicator facilitates change among the grieving community, his/her role must not be to offer timeless or eternal solutions. In fact, the development communicator does not offer any solutions. His/her role is to be a catalyst of change. His/her role is to address every situation as being different from the other. As Brueggemann asserts, "no prophet ever sees things under the aspect of eternity. It is always partisan ... always for the moment, always for the concrete community." (Brueggemann 16) Finally, the development communicator must realize that he/she is not the cause of change but only an important agent of that change. As a result he/she must acknowledge his/her reliance on the ultimate source of liberation that transcends him/her.

The prophetic action required in liberating the African woman must be grounded in and operable within the context of the two pillars of development, namely, individual initiative and institutional support (Anand & Amartyak 1996: 27) and grounded in theory of dialogic communication, advocacy and development. It is worthy of note that the theory of dialogic communication, rooted in Martin Buber's *I and Thou* and Paolo Freire's *Pedagogy of the Oppressed* are grounded in their religious beliefs. Both Buber and Freire have come to be respected within interdisciplinary circles for their contribution to dialogic communication, ethics and development. Hence, religious convictions have a significant role in the literature of liberation.

1. Individual Initiative[4]

The individual has the responsibility for his/her own development with the support of the institutions around him/her. Some ways that an individual takes initiative to develop himself/herself are the following:

- Awareness of one's situation and the possibilities for progress. Many African women are already conscious of the subservient and undignified way in which they are treated by men and their culture. This consciousness has been facilitated through various means: religion, migration, education, and women groups. The desire of women to liberate themselves from the indignity of any kind is particularly evident in the Charter of the Women of South Africa. Today, South Africa has a national policy that guarantees the rights of women against discrimination based on sex.
- Dialogue: awareness of one's situation should lead to dialogue with other people (including family members and other authority figures). This may involve the assertion of one's rights (without being aggressive). Through dialogue people make a genuine effort to change a situation "within a conversational context that seeks not violence, but concern for the other and calls for responsible action. (Arnett and Arneson 1999, 302) This means that women must not be afraid to speak directly to their husbands, community leaders, traditional authorities, and political or religious leaders as partners in the development of their societies. They should do so on the basis of subjects (I–You and not I–It) as Buber explains. (Buber 1970, 54-56).
- Forming or aligning with existing groups that share a person's vision for change/development. In this domain, it is important to mention the many women's movements that are fighting to ensure that national and international treaties on the status of women are

[4] This section is inspired by Paolo Friere's *Pedagogy of the Oppressed*, 1973 and Martin Buber's *I and Thou*, 1970.

respected. Examples of such movements are 31st December Women's Movement in Ghana, the BAKANJA in Eastern and Central Africa, and the Pan African Women's Liberation Organization in Uganda.

- Education: education opens doors to development. For example, to avoid being misled, an uneducated person may enroll in a literacy program in order to gain the basics of reading and writing. Or, a school drop-out could decide to go back to a vocational school to learn some vocational skills, etc. Education can also help people to learn different ways of dealing with their differences without resorting to violence. Above all, education that liberates a person must be a means by which a person is assisted to "deal critically and creatively with reality and discover how to participate in the transformation of their world." (Freire 1973,15) To realize this kind of education, government and professionals in education (teachers) as well as parents must ensure that the educational system prepares young African men and women through a "relational, reflective, and experiential way of knowing" so that by critical reflection on their experience they will be "able to discover and name their own story and vision." (Groome 1980, 147)
- Employment: with employment comes income and this is a major source of empowerment. When a person earns income from his/her job the person is less likely to be dependent on others.

2. Institutional Support

Institutional support must come from all institutions that have a stake in promoting human rights. These institutions must include the family, chieftaincy, churches or places of worship, the local and national government, as well as international bodies that defend human rights.

- The Family: Nuclear and Extended

In many African societies the family extends beyond the nuclear family (father, mother and children) to the extended family (uncles, aunts, grandparents, clan members, etc). In Africa, the family was a major source of values and support for individuals. Families must continue to play this role even as the society undergoes change due to urbanization, education and the introduction of the money economy. The institutional support from the family can come in the form of parents refusing to have their daughters genitally mutilated, or family members saying positive things about their sister- or daughter-in-law, or by women speaking out about their experiences to other people within or outside the family who are capable of assisting them to overcome the problems.

- National and local authority

The role of national and local authorities such as the governments at the national and local levels is to enact policies and ensure the proper execution of policies for the benefit of citizens. Their most fundamental role in civic society has to be the desire for justice for all the citizens they serve.

- Religious Institutions/leaders

In many respects, Christian and Muslim religions and leaders have replaced the traditional authority such as the custodian of the earth/land or diviner in many African societies. Before the advent of Christianity and Islam, these figures performed religious as well as legal functions. The diviner offered sacrifice on behalf of his people and settled disputes that arose between or among his people. Today these roles have largely been taken over by the Christian and Muslim leaders. As a source of institutional support for development, religious leaders must create environments where people can go to have their religious and human needs met, have their conflicts resolved and even to have someone to listen to their problems.

- NGOs and International Organizations

Non-governmental organizations at local, national or international levels play an important role in development. They empower many segments of the population in Africa by providing micro-credits, grants, donations, counseling services and expert advice to individuals and groups. To accomplish their role effectively, representatives of NGOs should respect the local culture and endeavor to work in collaboration with the communities they serve.

At all these levels—individual or institutional—the role of the development communicator must be prophetic in terms of ability to critique social situations and energize the grieving populations in the hope that things can change for the better.

Conclusion

This paper has considered prophetic imagination as a paradigm for the role of development communication in liberating women in Africa. As prophetic imagination, the development communicator plays the role of facilitator of a "consciousness that is a genuine alternative" to the *status quo* of traditional subjection of women to men in many African societies.

This paper expressed conviction that social constructs of reality can and should be changed in order to allow people – every human person – to develop and become who he/she is meant to become. The liberation sought must be one that enables women to participate in the development agenda of Africa through active involvement in politics, education, and employment outside the home as well as to live in environments in which they are safe from sexual harassment, forced marriage or genital mutilation. Liberating women in Africa should not be liberation for licentious or irresponsible life-styles but liberation for productive development of their human potential that contributes to the transformation of their society.

Finally, liberating the 'mistress' in Africa in order to grant her a new identity as woman (self-determining subject in collaboration with men) and an active agent in the development agenda of Africa must be an ongoing process without which society may become complacent or stagnant.

References

Agunga, Robert. *Developing the Third World: A Communication Approach.* Commack, NY: Nova Science Publishers, 1997.

Anand, Sudhir & Amartyak, Sen. *Sustainable Human Development: Concepts and Priorities.* UNDP/ODS. New York, 1996.

Arnett, Ronald C. & Arneson, Pat. *Dialogic Civility in a Cynical Age: Community, Hope, and Interpersonal Relationships.* Albany, NY: SUNY, 1999.

Berlo, David K. *The Process of Communication: An Introduction to Theory and Practice.* San Francisco: Rinchart Press, 1960.

Boserup, Ester. *Women's Role in Economic Development.* London: Earthscan Publications, 1970/1995.

Brueggemann, Walter. *The Prophetic Imagination.* Minneapolis: Fortress Press, 2001.

Buber, Martin. *I and Thou.* New York: Simon & Shuster, 1970.

Bunch, Charlotte. "The Intolerable Status Quo: Violence against Women and Girls" in *The Progress of Nations*: 41-45, 1997.

Charlton, Sue Ellen M. *Women in Third World Development.* Boulder and London: Westview Press, 1984.

Cutrufelli, Maria Rosa. *Women of Africa: Roots of Oppression.* Translated by Nicolas Romano. London: Zed Press, 1983.

Freire, Paolo. *Pedagogy of the Oppressed.* New York, NY: The Seabury Press, 1973.

Groome, Thomas. *Christian Religious Education: Sharing Our Story and Vision.* San Francisco: Jossey-Bass Publishers, 1980.

Hawkins, Sean. *Writing and Colonialism in Northern Ghana: The Encounter between the LoDagaa and "the World on Paper."* Toronto: University of Toronto Press, 2002.

Huston, Perdita. *Third World Women Speak Out.* New York: Praeger Press, 1979.

Kanogo, Tabitha. *African Womanhood in Colonial Kenya, 1900-50.* Athens, OH: Ohio University Press, 2005.

Kessey, Charles Boady. *Participatory Implementation: The Gender Dimension in the Implementation of Community-level Projects in Ghana.* Helsinki University Printing House, 2004.

Kruijer, Gerald J. *Development through Liberation: Third World Problems and Solutions*. Translated by Arnold Pomerans. Atlantic Highlands, NJ: Humanities Press International, 1987.

Lasswell. H.D. "The Structure and Function of Communication in Society," in L. Bryson(Ed.). *The Communication of Ideas*. New York: Harper and Brothers, 1948.

McCoy, Remigius F. *Great Things Happen: A Personal Memoir of the First Christian Missionary among the Dagaabas and Sissalas of northwest Ghana*. Montreal: The Society of Missionaries of Africa, 1988.

Melkote, Srinivas R. & Steeves, Leslie H. *Communication for Development in the Third World: Theory and Practice for Empowerment*. 2nd Edition. New Delhi: Sage Publications, 2001.

Mill, John Stuart. *The Subjection of Women*. New York: Prometheus Books, 1986 (1861).

Mody, Bella. (Ed). *International and Development Communication: A 21st Century Perspective*. Thousand Oaks: Sage Publications, 2003.

Mozammel, Masud & Schecter, Gailia. *Strategic Communication for Community Driven Development: A Practical Guide for Project managers and Communication Practitioners*. The World Bank, Washington, DC, 2005.

Muthien, Bernedette & Combrinck, Helene. *When Rights are wronged; Gender-based Violence & Human Rights in Africa*. Publication forthcoming in *Transnational Transgressions: African Women, Struggle and Transformation in Global Perspectives*. M. Bahati Kuumba and Monica Wjite (Eds).

Mutume, Gumisai. "African Women Ready to Lead," in *Africa Renewal*, UN Department of Public Information, vol. 20, No. 2, July, 2006.

Narayan, Deepa, Robert Chambers, Meera Kaul Shah and Patti Petesch. *Voices of the Poor: Crying Out for Change*. New York, NY: Oxford University Press, 2000.

Oboe, Christine. *African Women: Their Struggle for Economic Independence*. London: Zed Press, 1980.

Snyder, Leslie B. "Development Communication Campaigns," in *International and Development Communication: A 21st Century Perspective*. Edited by Bella Mody. Thousand Oaks, CA: Sage Publications, 2003.

Steeves, Leslie, H. "Liberation, Feminism, and Development," in *Communication Theory* 11(4), 397-414, 2001.

Steeves, Leslie H. "Development Communication as Marketing, Collective Resistance, and Spiritual Awakening: A Feminist Critique" in *International and Development Communication A 21st Century Perspective,* Edited by Bella Mody. Thousand Oaks: Sage Publications, 2003.

Suom-Dery, Eugene. *Family as Subject of Moral Education in the African Context: Incarnating Christian Ethics among the Dagara of North-western Ghana.* Hamburg, Germany: Verlag Dr. Kovac, 2000.

Taniguchi, Makoto. "Participatory Development: A Key Element in Development Strategies for the 1990s" in *Change: Threat or Opportunity for Human Progress?* Edited by Uner Kirdar. United Nations, New York, 1992.

Walker, Cheryl. *Women and Resistance in South Africa.* London: Onyx Press, 1982.